Slices of Orange

Slices of
ORANGE

Great Games and Performers in Syracuse University Sports History

Sal Maiorana *and* Scott Pitoniak

SYRACUSE UNIVERSITY PRESS

First Edition 2005
   06 07 08 09 10   6 5 4 3 2

All photographs courtesy of the Syracuse University Athletics Department.

The paper used in this publication meets the minimum requirements of
American National Standard for Information Sciences—Permanence of Paper
for Printed Library Materials, ANSI Z39.48-1984.∞™

Library of Congress Cataloging-in-Publication Data

Maiorana, Sal, 1962–
   Slices of orange : great games and performers in Syracuse University sports
history / Sal Maiorana and Scott Pitoniak.—1st ed.
       p.   cm.
   Includes bibliographical references.
   ISBN 0-8156-0844-6 (pbk. : alk. paper)
   1. Syracuse University—Sports—History.   I. Pitoniak, Scott.   II. Title.
GV691.S97M35 2005
796.04'30974766
2005030530

Manufactured in the United States of America

To Christine and our three children,
Taylor, Holden, and Caroline:
The Carrier Dome isn't big enough to hold
the amount of love I have for you.

—Sal Maiorana

To my home-team heroes,
Amy and Christopher:
Your dad loves you more than life itself.

—Scott Pitoniak

Sal Maiorana was born in Buffalo, New York, and earned a bachelor of arts degree in journalism at Buffalo State College. He has worked for the Associated Press and for the past nineteen years on the sports staff with the *Rochester Democrat and Chronicle*. He is also a regular contributor to numerous magazines and online sites and is the author of ten other books, including the two-volume history of the Buffalo Bills, *Relentless: The Hard-Hitting History of Buffalo Bills Football*. He has won numerous awards and citations for his work at the *Democrat and Chronicle*.

Scott Pitoniak is a native of Rome, New York, and a magna cum laude graduate of Syracuse University. He has spent the past quarter century as an award-winning sports columnist for the *Rochester Democrat and Chronicle*. He also teaches journalism at St. John Fisher College in Rochester, is the author of six regional best-selling books, and served as an associate editor and contributor to *The Encyclopedia of New York State*. Among his numerous honors, he was named one of the top-ten sports columnists in the United States by the Associated Press Sports Editors, he was inducted into the Newhouse School of Public Communications Hall of Fame and the Frontier Field Walk of Fame, and he was selected as a torchbearer during the 2002 Winter Olympics.

Contents

Illustrations

Acknowledgments

The authors would like to thank the following people and organizations, without whom the publication of this book would not have been possible:

Syracuse University Press, specifically director Peter Webber, assistant to the director Ellen Goodman, and copy editor Annette Wenda, for taking this idea and running with it. Syracuse University Sports Information director Sue Cornelius Edson, who along with her coworkers Pete Moore, Kerrin Perniciaro, and Marlene Ouderkirk provided invaluable assistance in selecting the photos to illustrate the book.

The athletes, coaches, and administrators who provided insight into the special moments we've attempted to chronicle.

Introduction

There are athletic achievements that stand the test of time—perform-ances that years or even decades later bring a smile or, in some cases, a grimace to a fan's face. They are indelible moments that, when strung together, give you a sense of history.

While backpedaling through more than a half century's worth of Syracuse University's sporting life, we discovered an abundance of transcendent events. Paring the list to just twenty-five memorable per-formances and performers was a daunting task—at times about as easy as tackling Jim Brown in the open field or stopping Sherman Douglas on a fast break.

But we've given it the old college try, and we believe you'll find this collection a representative sample of the most unforgettable moments in Orange history.

In these pages you will:

• be transported back to the night in dusty Manley Field House when Dave Bing soared above the competition with thirty-nine points and twenty-five rebounds, once more elevating SU basketball to new heights;

• learn how Heisman Trophy winner Ernie Davis almost missed the biggest game in SU football history because of a fluky but excruciatingly painful hamstring injury;

• recall when Jim Brown and Gerry McNamara put up forty-three points apiece in a single game—Big Jim on the chewed-up grass at ol' Archbold Stadium and G-Mac on a mile-high basketball court in Denver;

• experience the "McNificence" of quarterback Donovan McNabb during the waning seconds of a heart-stopping victory over Virginia Tech in the Carrier Dome;

• thrill once more to the half-court, buzzer-beating, game-winning heave by Pearl Washington;

• discover how extraordinary genes have played a prominent role in the SU lacrosse dynasty—from the father-and-son combination of Roy Simmons Sr. and Jr. to game-revolutionizing twin brothers Paul and Gary Gait and the record-setting Powell clan;

• relive the agony of defeat when Indiana University guard Keith Smart's jumper found nothing but net just before the final horn of the 1987 NCAA basketball title game;

• be reminded how Georgetown University basketball coach John Thompson rubbed salt in Syracuse's wound when he announced that Manley Field House was "officially closed" after his Hoyas snapped SU's fifty-seven-game home-court winning streak, the moment that launched one of the fiercest rivalries in all of college sports;

• journey not that far back in time to the memorable 2003 NCAA basketball title game against Kansas in New Orleans when Jim Boeheim finally exorcised some persistent ghosts in the very same building where sixteen years earlier Smart had plunged a dagger into his heart; and

• come to understand the David-versus-Goliath magnitude of the football upset the Orangemen sprang on top-ranked Nebraska during the autumn of 1984. In the noisy SU locker room following that game, defensive end Tim Green bellowed above the din: "This is why I came to Syracuse. I wanted to be able to experience moments like this one."

And we wanted you to be able to experience these moments, too, through the eyes of the performers who made them so special. It is our fervent hope that you have as much fun reliving these slices of Orange sports history as we had writing them.

Enjoy.

Slices of Orange

Book of Saints

1

Singh's Slings Sink Cornell

October 15, 1938
Archbold Stadium
Syracuse, New York

He is often a forgotten figure in Syracuse University sports history, but Wilmeth Sidat-Singh's dual sport career as a football and basketball star was among the most storied in Orange annals. At long last, his contributions were recognized in 2005 when his basketball number, 19, was retired, yet it was on the gridiron at Archbold Stadium where he enjoyed perhaps his finest moment, leading a come-from-behind victory over Cornell.

While strolling across campus one afternoon during the autumn of 1936, Roy Simmons Sr. stopped to take in an intramural football game. The Syracuse University varsity football coach couldn't help but notice a quick-footed, pinpoint-passing young man playing quarterback for one of the dormitory squads. Simmons soon realized that the signal caller was none other than Wilmeth Sidat-Singh, star of the Orange basketball team. Although it was just a game of touch, it quickly became apparent to Simmons's trained eye that Sidat-Singh was as adept with an oblong ball as he was with a round one. After watching the sophomore deliver one tight spiral after another, Simmons decided to do a little pitching of his own.

"I went over there and stopped the game," the coach recalled during an interview in the mid-1970s. "I said, 'Singh, you don't belong here. You belong down on that other field with the varsity. With your

1

ability you could make the football team, and you could make it with ease.' "

Sidat-Singh, who had played football at DeWitt Clinton High School in Harlem, was intrigued by what Simmons had to say. The following season, he took the coach up on his offer. Neither he nor Simmons would be disappointed.

During the third game of his senior season, Sidat-Singh ignited one of the most stirring comebacks in Syracuse sports history, adding to a two-sport legacy that only in recent years has been dusted off and given its proper due.

The greatness that caught Simmons's eye during that touch football game was there for the college football world to see during the final nine minutes of the 1937 clash with upstate rival Cornell at Archbold. With twenty-five thousand spectators looking on during an unusually hot October day, the visiting Big Red stormed to a 10-0 lead and seemed in complete control as the minutes began ticking away in the fourth quarter.

To the glee of Cornell rooters and the ire of Orange fans, the Big Red band repeatedly played its alma mater, "Far above Cayuga's Waters." A Syracuse writer equated the song to a funeral dirge. But Sidat-Singh would not allow his team's hopes for victory to die.

Within a period of six minutes, the sinewy six-foot 190-pounder would complete six passes for 150 yards and three touchdowns to give the Orangemen a 19-17 victory.

Grantland Rice, perhaps the most famous sportswriter of all time, was at the game and couldn't help but gush, calling it the most exciting college football game he had ever covered. Employing the flowery prose of the day, Rice wrote: "A new forward-pass hero slipped in front of the great white spotlight of fame at Syracuse today. The phenomenon of the rifle-shot event went beyond Sid Luckman and Sammy Baugh. His name is Wilmeth Sidat-Singh."

Singh's feat was a headline writer's dream. "Singh's Slings Sink Cornell" read one. "It Don't Mean a Thing If It Ain't Got That Singh" read another.

The Orangemen finally removed the zero from their side of the scoreboard midway through the fourth quarter when Singh flung a 35-yard touchdown pass to Harold "Babe" Ruth to cut the deficit to 10-6.

The TD stoked the Orange faithful, but their hopes were quickly dashed when Cornell's Kenny Brown returned the Syracuse kickoff 94 yards to go up 17-6.

"He seemed to carry all Orange hopes of victory with him," SU captain James Bruett recalled of that demoralizing return.

But Sidat-Singh would come to the rescue again. He returned the ensuing kickoff deep into Big Red territory, and two snaps later he connected with Ruth in the end zone again to slice Cornell's lead to 17-12 with roughly three minutes to play.

"We kicked off to Cornell, and they were trying to run out the clock," recalled Duffy Daugherty, an SU lineman on that team who would go on to earn College Football Hall of Fame honors after an illustrious coaching career at Michigan State.

"They ran a buck up the middle. I remember I was playing guard, and as Vinnie Eichler was being tackled, our left end, Phil Allen, yelled, 'Here Vinnie,' and Eichler mistakenly tossed our man a lateral. The next play, Sidat-Singh threw a pass to Allen in the end zone for the winning touchdown."

Rice's syndicated account of the game was carried in virtually every major newspaper in the United States. It wasn't merely the fact that SU had upset the top football team in the East, but rather the spectacular manner of the comeback that made it such a huge sports story.

"We had a great group of men, and they were all great competitors," Daugherty said. "We always felt we had a chance to win that game. We were moving the ball well. It was a hot Indian summer day, and we could sense that the Cornell team was getting tired and we were coming on strong. Of course, you have to have some breaks. And Sidat-Singh did a masterful job of throwing the football. It was just a great thrill."

That game would be the highlight of Sidat-Singh's football career and should have opened the door to a career as a professional quarterback. But racist policies did what few opponents on the football field had been able to do—stop Sidat-Singh cold. From 1934 to 1946, the National Football League bylaws included a clause banning black players.

Sidat-Singh had become familiar with racial injustice during both his college football and his college basketball careers. A year before Sidat-Singh's heroics against Cornell, Sam Lacy, a prominent African American newspaper reporter, broke the story that the young man was black, not Hindu as his surname indicated. Sidat-Singh had been born Wilmeth Webb in Washington, D.C., in 1917 and had adopted the new surname after his mother, Pauline, married Dr. Samuel Sidat-Singh, a prominent Harlem physician who had emigrated from India.

Lacy's story ran a week before Syracuse was scheduled to play at the University of Maryland. Like many schools south of the Mason-Dixon line, Maryland had a policy of not playing any home games against teams with African American players on their roster.

Sadly, SU officials kowtowed to Maryland's demands and played the game without Sidat-Singh.

"My sister and my husband went up there that day," Sidat-Singh's aunt, Adelaide Webb Henley, recalled in a February 2001 interview with the *New York Daily News*. "Wilmeth was just sitting there, with his head down, so embarrassed and humiliated."

Perhaps none of Sidat-Singh's teammates was more torn before that game than SU receiver Marty Glickman. On the eve of the 400-yard relay race at the 1936 Olympics in Berlin, American officials scratched the eighteen-year-old Glickman from the competition because he was Jewish. They feared his presence would offend German chancellor Adolph Hitler. Glickman contemplated sitting out the Maryland game as a show of support for his friend and roommate, but chose not to. It was a decision that would haunt Glickman for the rest of his life.

Sidat-Singh wound up leading the SU basketball team to a 14-4 record his senior season, but he would be forced to deal with racial injustice once more. Naval Academy officials said their team would not play any squad that included African Americans. Once again, SU hierarchy caved in to the discriminatory demands, and Sidat-Singh was forced to sit on the sidelines.

Rice's comparisons of the SU star to NFL all-time greats Luckman and Baugh indicate that Sidat-Singh had the potential to become a Hall of Famer, too, more than a half-century before present-day African American stars such as Donovan McNabb, Michael Vick, and Daunte Culpepper have put an end once and for all to racist arguments that blacks aren't qualified to play quarterback.

With the door to a professional football career bolted shut, Sidat-Singh began carving his professional sports niche in basketball. Playing for the Harlem-based New York Rens, he teamed with several men who would become black pioneers when the National Basketball Association began play in the late 1940s.

Sidat-Singh certainly would have joined them had his life not been cut tragically short at age twenty-five during a World War II training mission in 1943. Sidat-Singh was among black America's best and brightest who signed up for the Tuskegee Airmen, an all-black fighter squadron whose success in shooting down Nazi planes during the war led to the desegregation of the U.S. armed forces.

An aspiring doctor, Sidat-Singh earned his wings quickly and was ready to head off to the European theater. But during a training mission over Lake Huron, the engines on his P-40 pursuit plane began to malfunction, and he was forced to parachute. When he hit the frigid waters, he became entangled in the ropes of his parachute and drowned. Six weeks later, his body was found, and he was buried in Arlington National Cemetery.

On February 26, 2005, during halftime of the Providence-Syracuse game at the Carrier Dome, Sidat-Singh's number 19 basketball jersey was officially retired by his alma mater. His jersey now hangs near the Dome's rafters along with those of former SU basketball greats Dave Bing, Vic Hanson, Pearl Washington, and Sherman Douglas. As Syracuse Post-Standard *columnist Sean Kirst wrote: "Raising his jersey, then, is intended both as a tribute and as a means of healing some old wounds." The ceremony was the brainchild of Larry Martin, an assistant to the vice president at SU. "When we won that national championship [in basketball in 2003], and everyone was offering credit for the victory, I thought of Wilmeth Sidat-Singh and how he paved the way for generations of African-Americans at Syracuse," Martin said. "I think this will be a fitting tribute for an extraordinary individual who up until this point has almost been hidden from us." Yvonne Jenson, one of Sidat-Singh's cousins, was pleased that more than a half century later a wrong had been righted. "For him to go down in Syracuse history," she told the* Post-Standard, *"is a most comforting thing."*

Orange Slice—Marty Glickman

He was the first in a long line of famous sportscasters who got their start at Syracuse University. But long before he became known as the voice of the New York Giants, Knicks, and Jets, Marty Glickman made his mark as an athlete.

Blessed with incredible speed, Glickman was recruited to run track and play football at SU. He earned All-American honors as a sprinter and was selected to compete on the U.S. track and field team at the 1936 Olympics in Berlin. He was scheduled to run a leg on the 4 x 100-yard relay team but was scratched at the last minute because he was Jewish and U.S. officials feared his presence would offend German chancellor Adolf Hitler.

It was a wound that never completely healed, and when Glickman visited Germany in 1985 as part of a tribute to the great Jesse Owens, he wrote:

> As I walked into the stadium, I began to get so angry. I began to get so mad. It shocked the hell out of me that this thing of forty-nine years ago could still evoke this anger. . . . I was cussing. . . . I was really amazed at myself, at this feeling of anger. Not about the German Nazis . . . that was a given. But the anger at [Olympic officials] Avery Brundage and Dean Cromwell for not allowing an eighteen-year-old kid to compete in the Olympic Games just because he was Jewish. They took my dream away from me.

Demoralized by the anti-Semitic decision, Glickman returned to Syracuse where he turned his athletic attentions to football. His blazing speed served him well on the gridiron. Starting three seasons at running back and end, Glickman helped the Orangemen rebound from a 1-7 record in 1936 to 5-2-1 and 5-3 won-lost marks in succeeding years.

One of his most memorable games occurred in 1937, when he rushed for more than 100 yards as SU handed eastern powerhouse Cornell its only defeat of the season.

In a 1938 victory against Maryland, Glickman broke free on an 80-yard touchdown run—the fifth longest in school history.

Glickman overcame an early-life stuttering problem by taking speech lessons as a child, and he went on to become one of the most recognizable and respected sportscasters in the United States during the 1950s and '60s.

Glickman used terminology in describing basketball games that lives on more than a half century later. *The key, the lane, the top of the circle, the mid-court stripe, between the circles,* and *swish*—they were all coined by Glickman.

Although he spent twenty-one years calling Knicks' basketball games and sixteen years doing play-by-play for the Jets, he was most closely associated with the football Giants, whose games he broadcast from 1948 to 1971. He later became the broadcast coach for NBC. Glickman died in 2001 at age eighty-three.

Marty Glickman

Date of birth: August 14, 1917

Hometown: Bronx, New York

Honors: Is a member of the Basketball Hall of Fame, the New York City Sports Hall of Fame, and the New York City Basketball Hall of Fame. . . . Was the first winner of Springfield's coveted Curt Gowdy Media Award.

Achievements: Qualified for a spot on the United States 4 x 100-yard relay team in the 1936 Summer Olympics at Berlin. . . . Played three years of varsity football and also captained the SU track team. . . . Mentored some of America's finest broadcasters, including Marv Albert and the late Johnny Most.

2

Colgate Suffers a Brown-out

November 17, 1956   *It only seems appropriate that Jim Brown,*
Archbold Stadium   *the greatest player in Syracuse's storied*
Syracuse, New York   *football history, is responsible for the*
school's greatest gridiron performance, a
forty-three-point explosion against up-
state rival Colgate.

The Orangemen were riding a five-game winning streak heading into their final scheduled game of the 1956 season, but skeptics remained.

Although senior Jim Brown, a chiseled six-foot-two, 212-pound Adonis, had been sprinting around, over, and through everybody he had faced that autumn, some college football observers believed Syracuse and its unstoppable number 44 were ripe to be had.

Those doubts were expressed in print just two days before the 'Cuse was ready to host Upstate New York neighbor Colgate in venerable Archbold Stadium when the national college football writer for the Associated Press predicted a Red Raiders upset. The column was carried in the sports sections of virtually every newspaper in the country.

By the time that Saturday's Syracuse game ended, it was difficult to discern who was more embarrassed: the Colgate defenders who futilely attempted to keep Brown out of their end zone or the prognosticator who failed to recognize the greatness and the fury of the young man who would become the standard by which all future running backs would be measured.

Many had worn the number 44 football jersey before Jim Brown arrived on campus in 1954, but the number became a legacy thanks to the distinction with which Brown, shown here in the 1957 Cotton Bowl against Texas Christian University, played during his three years at Syracuse.

As the sun set, quite appropriately orange, that late November afternoon, the scoreboard read: Syracuse 61, Colgate 7.

It could just as easily have read, "Jim Brown 43, Colgate 7," because that's how many points the young man from Manhasset, Long Island, scored in his final game in the concrete bowl known as Ol' Archie.

Brown certainly gave the packed house of forty thousand spectators a parting gift they would never forget, scoring on touchdown runs of 1, 15, 50, 8, 19, and 1 yards. He also kicked seven extra points and, for good measure, intercepted a pass and caused a fumble while playing defensive back to stymie two potential scoring drives.

"He probably could have scored 10 touchdowns without too much additional effort," Val Pinchbeck, the late Syracuse sports information director, noted that day.

The forty-three points established a major college record for individual scoring that lasted nearly three decades. It also put an exclamation point on Brown's campaign for All-American honors and earned the Orangemen an invitation to the Cotton Bowl.

Interestingly, leading up to the game, Colgate coach Hal Lahar was concerned that the run-oriented Orangemen might pull a fast one and attempt to pass the ball more often than usual. As a result, he spent extra time that week preparing for an increased aerial assault.

It was time poorly spent because SU stayed true to its grind-it-out, grind-'em-up approach, rushing for 511 yards while passing just seven times for 99 yards. Brown led the way, accumulating 197 yards on twenty-two carries—a remarkable 8.9 yards per carry—and also caught one pass for 13 yards. The rushing performance enabled him to eclipse the school marks for most yards and points in a season. It also enabled the Orangemen to improve their won-lost record to 7-1, the best mark by an SU football team since 1923. The record-setting day included a new mark for most points by a team in the series, surpassing the total accumulated by Colgate in a 58-0 victory in 1893.

Though the college football writer from the Associated Press might have been caught by surprise by arguably the finest individual performance in Orange football history, fans in Syracuse weren't. They had grown accustomed to such athletic heroics by the talented but temperamental young man known as the "Manhasset Mauler."

Brown's sporting talents were readily apparent in high school, where he excelled in football, basketball, baseball, lacrosse, and track and field. He established himself as Manhasset's all-time scoring leader in basketball, and after throwing two no-hitters in baseball he attracted interest from the New York Yankees. Swayed by Syracuse alum Kenny Malloy who had become his mentor, Brown enrolled at Syracuse. Remarkably, he did not receive an athletic scholarship until his sophomore year when it became obvious even to stubborn football coach Ben Schwartzwalder that Brown was a talent unlike any he had ever seen before.

There were numerous bumps in the road along the way as Brown considered leaving school over what he viewed as bigotry on the part of certain SU coaches. But Malloy convinced him to stick it out, and so began the legend of number 44.

During his junior year at Syracuse, Brown played varsity football, basketball, lacrosse, and track and field. As good as he was in football, some regard him as an even better lacrosse player, and there was talk that if he had played basketball his senior year, SU would have faced Kansas and its seven-foot-one center, Wilt Chamberlain, in the national championship game.

One of Brown's greatest feats occurred during the spring of his junior year when he competed in two different sports on the same day at Archbold Stadium. He wound up finishing first in the high jump and discus and second in the javelin to account for 13 points in a victory against Colgate in track and field. Later that same day, he helped the Orangemen defeat Army in lacrosse.

Brown wound up becoming the school's first four-sport letterman since Jim Konstanty in the mid-1940s. (Konstanty would wind up becoming a star reliever and the 1950 National League most valuable player with the Philadelphia Phillies.)

Despite his brilliance in other sports, football would become the game that Brown was best known for, and at Syracuse he clearly saved his best for last, helping the Orange program shake off the lingering effects of an embarrassing 61-6 loss it had suffered against Alabama four years earlier.

Brown served notice in the first game of the 1956 season, rushing for 154 yards and catching a 24-yard touchdown pass from Jim Ridlon in a 26-12 victory against Maryland, a national powerhouse.

Later that season, in a matchup against eastern standard-bearer Army, Brown displayed his two-way prowess. He rushed for 125 yards and set up Ridlon's touchdown with a 37-yard burst in the second quarter. Then, with SU clinging to a 7-0 lead late in the final period, Brown made three tackles during a goal-line stand to preserve the victory.

After that game, legendary Army coach Earl Blaik compared Brown to former cadet Heisman Trophy winners Doc Blanchard and Glenn Davis. "He has the speed and power to be Mr. Inside and Mr. Outside combined," Blaik said, referring to the football nicknames sportswriters had pegged on Blanchard and Davis.

The Monday following his explosive performance against Colgate, Brown was named first-team All-America—the first time a running back from the school was ever accorded that honor.

"We had a good, big and fast line that made things easy for me," he said, deflecting praise. "I shudder when I think of running against my own linemen."

Although his line mates were very good, they, too, would no doubt have had difficulty stopping Brown's punishing runs. Yes, they had opened holes and contributed to his success, but, to a man, they knew that much of Brown's yardage was gained after he had absorbed a hit.

As good as his effort was against Colgate, Brown's performance against Texas Christian University in the Cotton Bowl that followed may have been even better. Though the Horned Frogs won, 28-27, Brown rushed for 132 yards and scored 21 points.

"The headlines should have read, `TCU 28, Jim Brown U. 27,' " said Ron Luciano, a former All-American offensive lineman at SU who went on to become one of the best-known umpires in Major League Baseball history. "Jim was a one-man wrecking crew that day. The rest of us were just along for the ride."

Brown's legacy at SU didn't end when he graduated and became a superstar with the Cleveland Browns of the National Football League. With the Browns he became the NFL's all-time leading rusher with 12,312 yards, and his standard stood nearly two decades until Walter Payton surpassed it in 1984. Brown played a role in convincing 1961 Heisman Trophy winner Ernie Davis to follow him to Syracuse, and Floyd Little would, in turn, continue the tradition after Davis left. The three men would combine to make the number 44 jersey synonymous with football greatness at the 'Cuse.

Orange Slice—Ben Schwartzwalder

Ben Schwartzwalder balked when one of his longtime mentors nudged him to apply for the head football coach's job at Syracuse University after the 1948 season.

"I'm not interested in Syracuse," said Schwartzwalder, who was having considerable success coaching football at tiny Muhlenberg (Pennsylvania) College. "Syracuse is a graveyard for football coaches."

Football coach Ben Schwartzwalder gazes at a schedule for the 1956 season. Of note is the November 17 Colgate game because on that afternoon at Archbold Stadium Jim Brown scored an NCAA single-game record forty-three points.

A few weeks later, the young coach had a change of heart after the president of Muhlenberg called him into his office and told him that he was doing too good of a job and that other schools in the Mid-Atlantic Conference were complaining about it.

"You can't win over half your games," the president told him. "So if you're going to stay at Muhlenberg, we don't want you to win over half your games."

Just to make sure his ears weren't deceiving him, the incredulous Schwartzwalder asked the president to repeat himself. He did, and Schwartzwalder informed him that he would immediately begin looking for another job.

Suddenly, the opening at Syracuse didn't seem like such a bad option after all.

Schwartzwalder applied and was hired by longtime SU athletic director Lew Andreas. The news was not widely hailed in Syracuse. The Orangemen were coming off a 1-8 record—the program's worst finish in fifty-six years—and although Schwartzwalder had gone 25-5 in three seasons at Muhlenberg, he was hardly the "name" coach SU fans had hoped for.

"The alumni wanted a big-name coach," the droll Schwartzwalder said years later, "and they wound up with a long-name coach."

In time, though, Schwartzwalder would become a household name in more than just his own household. And a Syracuse program that had mustered a mere eleven wins in its previous forty games would reach the Everest of college football with a national championship in 1959.

During ol' Ben's twenty-five-year reign, the Orangemen went 153-91-3 and made seven bowl appearances. His teams recorded twenty-two consecutive nonlosing seasons and churned out a long line of outstanding running backs, including Jim Brown, Heisman Trophy winner Ernie Davis, Floyd Little, and Larry Csonka.

A paratrooper in World War II, Schwartzwalder earned a Bronze Star, a Silver Star, and a Purple Heart for his heroics on D day and during the Battle of the Bulge. Slowly but surely, the coach with the trademark crew cut and the stern countenance built the program in his tough image.

"When you think of a hard-nosed, old-school football coach, you think of Ben Schwartzwalder," said Dick MacPherson, who would follow in his footsteps years later. "He was right out of central casting."

Success came slowly for Schwartzwalder at SU. Initially, school administrators allowed him only twelve football scholarships a year, less than half the number of other big-time schools. Competing for a national championship under those circumstances was the furthest thing from his mind. "I was hopeful of doing some business with Colgate," he recalled. "Maybe to catch Cornell. We had no further horizons at the moment."

Thanks to his persistent lobbying, the SU administration eventually upped the number of scholarships, and Ben's Boys began doing some business with the best teams in the East and nationwide.

By the late 1960s and early '70s, SU's football fortunes sagged once more. Several black players walked off the team in 1970 and branded Schwartzwalder a bigot. The deterioration of Archbold Stadium and a reduction in support by the administration resulted in a severe talent drain and a 2-9 record by Schwartzwalder's final team in 1973.

Despite the sad ending, he left his post as the winningest football coach in school history. He had guided the Orange program through its most glorious stretch and had resuscitated a place that had become a coaching graveyard.

Ben Schwartzwalder

Date of birth: June 2, 1909

Hometown: Point Pleasant, West Virginia

Honors: Was 1959 consensus national coach of the year.

Achievements: Played football at West Virginia under Greasy Neale. . . . At the time of his retirement he was one of only ten men who had coached at one school at least twenty-five years. . . . Served in World War II as a paratrooper and participated in 1944 D-day invasion. . . . Posted record of 25-5 in three years as head coach at Muhlenberg College. . . . Led Orange to only national championship in 1959. . . . All-time winningest SU coach. . . . Produced twenty-two consecutive years of nonlosing records.

SU career totals: Coaching record of 153-91-3.

3

Ben's Boys Reach Football's Summit

January 1, 1960   *The Orangemen proved the mettle of east-*
Cotton Bowl   *ern football in 1959 when they dominated*
Dallas, Texas   *all comers in winning their ten regular-*
season games, then traveled to the Cotton
Bowl on New Year's Day and whipped the
Longhorns in their own Texas backyard to
win the national championship.

He had pulled the Syracuse football program out of the abyss and had turned the Orangemen into a legitimate eastern power. No small feat, considering Ben Schwartzwalder had inherited a team that had gone 1-8 in 1948. But after suffering his third consecutive postseason defeat following the 1958 season—21-6 to Oklahoma in the Orange Bowl—patience began wearing thin in the Salt City.

There was a growing sentiment, particularly among some sports columnists in Syracuse and beyond, that Schwartzwalder was one of those good but not great coaches who couldn't win the big one.

A paratrooper who had survived jumps on D day and the Battle of the Bulge, Schwartzwalder shrugged off the scathing columns, telling one of his assistants, "I don't resent the criticism. The writers write what they see."

What the writers and everyone else would see in 1959 would be one of the greatest college football teams of all time.

Ol' Ben won the big one, as well as all the little ones leading up to it.

16

The 1959 team won all eleven of its games and won the football program's only national championship.

The '59ers totally dominated the college football landscape, winning all eleven of their games and becoming the first team in history to lead the nation in total offense (451.5 yards per game) and defense (96.2 yards per game). Led by their "Sizeable Seven" offensive line and a backfield known as the "Four Furies," the Orangemen atoned for previous bowl failures and struck a blow for eastern football with a decisive 23-14 victory against second-ranked Texas in the Cotton Bowl.

Their aggressive defense pitched five shutouts that season and held four different opponents to negative rushing yardage. That included a minus-88 rushing performance by Boston University. Led by future Heisman Trophy winner Ernie Davis, the offense did its part, too, leading the country in scoring with 39 points per game.

The Orangemen's talent was so abundant that during a nationally televised 38-6 annihilation of UCLA at the Los Angeles Coliseum, football Hall of Famer Red Grange told viewers: "If Syracuse's first team is the No. 1 team in the country, then their second team must be No. 2."

With most of his veteran players returning from a squad that went 8-2 in 1958, plus the addition of talented young players such as Davis and tackle John Brown, Schwartzwalder had a feeling that '59 could be something really special.

But his optimism was dulled somewhat a few weeks before the beginning of practices when his starting quarterback, Bob Thomas, was injured in a truck accident and lost for the season. That prompted the coach to shift halfback Gerhard Schwedes to quarterback in the opener against Kansas. He did fine as the Orangemen came from behind to beat the Jayhawks 35-21. But after reviewing the films, Schwartzwalder and his staff believed the team would be stronger with Schwedes back at running back. Dave Sarette stepped in at quarterback, and he, running backs Davis and Schwedes, and bruising fullback Art Baker formed a backfield that couldn't be stopped.

SU steamrolled its next five opponents by a combined score of 182-12, setting the stage for a crucial matchup with unbeaten Penn State in Happy Valley. The Orangemen held a seemingly commanding 20-6 lead midway through the second half, but the Nittany Lions stormed back on a kickoff return for a touchdown by Roger Kochman and a blocked punt. After their third score, Penn State opted to go for a two-point conversion that would have tied the game, but Kochman was stopped short by SU's Sizeable Seven line featuring Fred Mautino, Maury Youmans, Bob Yates, Bruce Tarbox, Al Bemiller, Roger Davis, and Gary Skonieczki. The Orangemen took the ensuing kickoff and ground out several first downs to run out the clock.

SU followed that win with a 71-0 rout of Colgate and a 46-0 thrashing of Boston University. That set up the nationally televised meeting with UCLA, which wound up being no contest.

"I think that was the game that showed we belonged," Youmans said.

A columnist from the *Los Angeles Times* was extremely impressed, issuing a warning to SU's next opponent, the Texas Longhorns in the Cotton Bowl. "Get ready to buck, boys," he wrote. "After watching Syracuse whack UCLA without working up a sweat, my advice to you is to go fishing on New Year's Day."

Still, not everyone was convinced that Syracuse was all it was cracked up to be. The Orangemen had never won a bowl game and were thought by some to be merely a paper champion heading down to Dallas.

In their previous postseason treks, Schwartzwalder had worked his team mercilessly. But this time he took it easy on his players, and Tarbox believes that made a huge difference. "I think Ben smartened up and realized he didn't have to run us into the ground to get us ready," he said.

Three days before the game, an incident occurred that threatened to turn SU's dream season into a nightmare. After practice, Davis, the team's best player, was taking part in a field-goal kicking contest with one of his teammates. As he attempted a field goal from 50 yards out, Davis felt a twinge in his leg and seconds later fell to the ground in excruciating pain. Trainers diagnosed him with a severely pulled hamstring, and his status for the game was doubtful. Davis watched the next two practices on crutches. But on the morning of the game, he told Schwartzwalder there was no way he was going to miss the Cotton Bowl.

The coaching staff figured Davis would be good for only a few plays. They figured wrong. Davis wound up scoring two touchdowns and a pair of two-point conversions to earn most valuable player honors.

On the second play from scrimmage at the SU 13-yard line, Sarette pitched to Schwedes who rolled right. Before he reached the sideline he lofted a pass downfield that hit Davis in stride. Despite being restricted by the pulled hammy, Davis outran his pursuers for an 87-yard touchdown—the longest reception in Cotton Bowl history.

"It was a halfback pitch, and I was supposed to get the ball," said Schwedes. "Ernie lined up as a flanker. The short man was covered, and Ernie was nowhere to be found. Ernie ran the wrong pattern, a post pattern. He was 40 yards downfield, seven or eight yards beyond the defensive back. I saw him and just flung it up there and he went and got it. Ernie ran the total opposite of what he was supposed to run and still outran them all. He was truly special."

A few possessions later Davis plunged in from the 1, and caught a two-point pass from Sarette to put SU up 15-0.

Texas cut the lead to 15-6 early in the third quarter on a 69-yard scoring pass from Bobby Lackey to Jack Collins, but the two-point conversion attempt failed.

The Longhorns were threatening again on their next possession, but Davis intercepted a pass and returned it 12 yards to the Texas 24. He then carried the ball to the 3-yard line, and four snaps later Schwedes scored. Davis caught another two-point conversion pass to put SU up by 17 and secure the national championship.

Davis's heroics wound up being overshadowed by the racist actions of several Longhorn players toward SU's three African American players, including Davis. Texas, which did not have any blacks on its roster, allegedly shouted racial epithets at SU tackle John Brown and spit in the face of SU fullback Art Baker. Brown said that Texas lineman Larry Stephens kept calling him a "big, black, dirty Nigger." At first, Brown turned a deaf ear to the taunting. Eventually, though, he decided he wasn't going to take it anymore and threw a punch at Stephens. Both benches emptied, and it was several minutes before order was restored.

Afterward, Brown told reporters he was willing to forgive Stephens. "That Texas boy was just excited," he said. "Let's forget it."

But others were not. Columnists throughout the country chastised Longhorn players, coaches, and officials for their bigoted behavior, and *Life* magazine focused on it in its coverage of the game.

"Sadly, it was a reflection of the times," Brown said years later. "I shrugged it off. I certainly wasn't going to allow it to distract me from what we had accomplished as a team."

Upon their return to Syracuse, the Orangemen were greeted by a throng of thousands at Hancock Field. Their Boys of Autumn had brought a national championship trophy back to central New York. No one was wondering if Schwartzwalder could win the big one anymore.

No Syracuse team in the four and a half decades since has matched the feat of the 1959 team. The closest the Orange came to winning another national championship was in 1987 when they went undefeated in the regular season, then played to a tie against Auburn in the Sugar Bowl, and finished fourth in both national polls.

Orange Slice—Ernie Davis

The life-size bronze statue stands tall on a granite pedestal outside the junior high school in Elmira, New York, that bears his name. It depicts

Ernie Davis inherited the number 44 jersey from Jim Brown and then broke most of Brown's school records, capping his brilliant career by winning the 1961 Heisman Trophy.

Ernie Davis, the one-time "Elmira Express," in a letterman's sweater, books in one hand, a football in the other. Nearly a half century after Davis's promising life was cut short by leukemia at age twenty-three, the sculpture serves as a reminder of a true hero who handled living and dying with remarkable dignity and grace.

In Elmira, where he won eleven varsity sports letters and All-American honors in football and basketball, and in Syracuse, where in

1961 he became the first African American to capture the prestigious Heisman Trophy, Davis's legacy remains strong.

After a superb athletic career at Elmira Free Academy in the mid- to late 1950s, Davis chose Syracuse over Notre Dame because he wanted to follow in the footsteps of his idol, Jim Brown, who had gone on to greatness with the Cleveland Browns of the National Football League.

No one was more pleased with Davis's decision than SU football coach Ben Schwartzwalder, who had made thirty recruiting visits to Elmira during the running back's senior season of high school.

Schwartzwalder saw the same football attributes in Davis that he had in Brown, so it wasn't surprising that the coach wound up issuing him Big Jim's old number—44.

Davis did the jersey proud, rushing for 2,386 yards during his three varsity seasons to eclipse Brown's school record. Though many have since gone on to surpass Davis's yardage totals at SU, no one has come close to equaling his career average of 6.63 yards per carry.

Davis wasted little time establishing himself as one of college football's impact players, averaging 7 yards per carry and scoring 8 touchdowns to lead the 1959 team to an 11-0 record and the national championship.

That season was capped by Davis's scintillating performance in a 23-14 victory over Texas in the Cotton Bowl. Despite nursing a severely pulled hamstring, Davis caught an 87-yard touchdown pass, scored on a 1-yard run, tallied two two-point conversions, and intercepted a pass in that victory.

Two years later, Davis concluded his brilliant college football career by winning the Heisman. Following the award ceremony at the Downtown Athletic Club in Manhattan, President John F. Kennedy asked to meet Davis. "I got to shake hands with him," Davis said later. "That was almost as big a thrill as winning the Heisman."

A month later, in January 1962, Davis experienced another big thrill when he turned down a huge contract offer from the Buffalo Bills of the American Football League and signed for less but still substantial money with the NFL's Browns. Davis was going to get an opportunity to play in the same backfield as his Syracuse predecessor, Jim Brown.

"The world was his oyster," recalled former SU offensive tackle John Brown, Davis's college roommate. "He had everything going for him at that time—looks, ability, character, charm, youth. Just about anyone would have traded places with him."

By September 1962, no one would have traded places with him. While prepping for the College All-Star Game against the Green Bay Packers in Buffalo, Davis began feeling run-down and noticed sores in his mouth and lumps on his neck. The symptoms persisted into the following week, and he checked into a hospital and was diagnosed with leukemia.

"He was bewildered at first, but he didn't complain," recalled former Browns owner Art Modell. "In fact, almost immediately, he began talking about how he was going to lick this thing."

That fall, his cancer went into remission but reoccurred at the beginning of 1963. Though discouraged by the news, Davis remained upbeat.

As John Brown put it:

> He would have been justified cursing: "Why me God? Why me?" But I never heard him bemoan his fate.
>
> I remember one time I came home from a particularly tough practice with the Browns. I was really down, really worried about making the team. Ernie sat there and listened to me bitch and tried to pick my spirits up. Suddenly, I realized how dumb I had been. I'm complaining about something as insignificant as making a football team in front of a guy battling for his life. That Ernie would listen to my little problems despite what he was facing was so typical of him. He always put the concerns of others ahead of himself.

On May 18, 1963, Davis died at Lakeside Hospital in Cleveland. His death touched the nation. His story transcended sports.

About ten thousand mourners, including most of the members of the Browns team for which he never played, attended his funeral at Elmira's Woodlawn Cemetery, where Mark Twain is also buried.

Jim Brown, one of the pallbearers, spoke eloquently about the young man whom he inspired and befriended:

> I've always felt the words "great" and "courage" have been overused and abused. I have never been one to take them idly. I say with the utmost sincerity: Ernie Davis, to me, was the greatest, most courageous person I've ever met. Though death is sad and often tragic—and these

elements were present in Ernie's death—his is not a sad story. He made our lives better, brighter, and fuller because we were privileged to know him. I find it difficult to believe he's gone. Maybe it's because I never heard him complain. The way he acted, he had me believing he'd make it.

Ernie Davis

Date of birth: December 14, 1939

Hometown: New Salem, Pennsylvania

Honors: Won 1961 Heisman Trophy. . . . MVP of 1960 Cotton Bowl. . . . Two-time All-American in 1960 and '61.

Achievements: Was first pick in 1961 NFL draft by Washington, was later traded to Cleveland, but never played, as he died of leukemia in 1963. . . . In high school he led Elmira Free Academy to a fifty-two-game winning streak in basketball. . . . Was a high school All-American in football and basketball and won eleven letters. . . . Holds SU records for average yards per carry for a game (15.7), season (7.8), and career (6.63).

SU career totals: 2,386 rushing yards, 392 receiving yards, 223 punt-return yards, 196 kickoff-return yards, 3,303 all-purpose yards, 35 touchdowns.

4

A Little Goes a Long Way

September 26, 1964
Archbold Stadium
Syracuse, New York

Saddled with the pressure of having to replace legendary running backs Jim Brown and Ernie Davis at Syracuse, Floyd Little proved he was up to the challenge when, in just his second varsity game, he scored five touchdowns and outplayed the great Gale Sayers of Kansas.

There were murmurs that the new kid was even better than the two Syracuse football players who had worn the number 44 jersey before him. And that was saying something since the first notable number 44 already owned six National Football League rushing titles and the second had won the Heisman Trophy.

But when Floyd Little struggled in his first varsity game at Boston College during the 1964 season opener, many Orange fans wondered what all the hype had been about. Perhaps the coaches, reporters, and fans had gotten their hopes too high. Perhaps Little wasn't cut from the same cloth as his famous predecessors, Jim Brown and Ernie Davis.

It didn't take long for the new kid on the block to allay such concerns. In game two of his varsity football career at Syracuse—his first in front of the home folks at Archbold Stadium—Little proved he was a worthy successor. It became obvious that this Little would go a long way.

Nationally ranked Kansas came to town that second week of the season, and most of the attention was focused on Gale Sayers, the Jayhawks senior running back who had earned All-American honors in 1963. The

25

Next in line to wear number 44 was Floyd Little who held alone
the all-time Syracuse record for touchdowns scored with forty-
six until Walter Reyes tied the mark in 2004.

future Pro Football Hall of Famer was expected to put on a show, and
the Orangemen were home underdogs.

However, that afternoon, Sayers wound up being upstaged by Little,
who turned in one of the greatest individual performances in SU athletic
history.

The bowlegged five-foot-eleven, 190-pound running back from New
Haven, Connecticut, wowed the crowd of twenty-eight thousand spectators by rushing for 159 yards and five touchdowns on just sixteen carries as the Orangemen crushed Kansas, 38-6. Sayers wasn't bad, gaining
84 yards on sixteen carries, but it was literally too Little that day.

Little scored on runs of 15, 1, 55, 3, and 19 yards. Amazingly, he
scored his five touchdowns during his final nine carries. For good mea-

sure, Little also caught two passes for 47 yards, and, tossing in his kick-off- and punt-return yardage, he advanced the football 254 yards in the game.

"That was the greatest performance by a back that I have ever seen," Jayhawks coach Jack Mitchell told reporters afterward—an extravagant compliment, considering Mitchell had been an eyewitness to Sayers's entertaining runs for two seasons.

It would not be the last compliment Little would receive from opposing coaches that autumn. After watching Little shred his defense, Penn State's legendary coach Joe Paterno noted: "The best defense against him, I have decided, is to have my old mother in Brooklyn say a novena." Army coach Paul Dietzel called Little "the greatest back in America."

No one would have argued with Dietzel if they had seen Little's 55-yard scoring jaunt against Kansas. He started off tackle, cut to the middle, and bounced off a number of defenders before reaching the end zone as Archbold erupted in glee.

"I think if you ran the play back slowly," said Ted Dailey, the Syracuse defensive line coach, "you'd find about eleven Kansas players either had a hand on him or a chance to tackle him."

Little would go on to rush for 828 yards and score twelve touchdowns as the Orangemen went 7-3 to earn a Sugar Bowl invitation. *Look* magazine named the SU running back to its All-American team, the only sophomore chosen. With Little, brutish fullback Jim Nance, and deerlike quarterback Wally Mahle running behind a big, tough offensive line, Syracuse led the nation in rushing with an average of 251 yards per game.

"Ol' Jim, then Ernie, now Floyd," coach Ben Schwartzwalder sighed one day in his office. "I think I ought to just pinch myself."

Little's father died of cancer when he was six, and his mother raised Floyd and his five siblings on meager earnings and welfare. Little struggled with his grades, failed the fifth grade, and when he finally graduated from high school at the age of nineteen his prospects were not promising. "In school they had me on a program of shop and physical education," he recalled. "When I got through I couldn't even read well. All I was trying to be was a custodian and I couldn't even handle that. But I was smart enough to know that I wasn't failing to get the job because I was black. I was failing because I couldn't read. I walked out of there knowing I'd never get the job, but I also knew I was going to come back and make it."

Little was told he had an IQ of eighty-five and that he would never make it in college. "I was told I was too dumb," he said. "But you try going without eating for two days and see how well you do on tests."

With the help of his high school coach, Dan Casey, Little was given hope. Casey wrote a letter to Notre Dame on Little's behalf, and the Irish football staff was so impressed with his football potential that they suggested he attend a prep school to raise his marks to an acceptable college level.

Little, under the impression that Notre Dame was footing the bill, enrolled at Bordentown Prep, a military school in New Jersey, and his life changed forever. Little captained the football, basketball, and track teams; was put in charge of a platoon; and his confidence and maturity—as well as his grades—soared.

While at Bordentown, forty-seven colleges expressed interest in bringing Little in to play football. During much of the process he was leaning toward South Bend because he had been told Notre Dame was paying his Bordentown tuition. When he learned that the military school was actually paying his way, he no longer felt obligated to repay a debt to the Irish.

And that's when Syracuse pounced on an opportunity. Schwartzwalder and Davis showed up on the front stoop of the Little home on a snowy Connecticut night to try to persuade Little to come to central New York. "There were three men in front, and standing behind them was this big guy in a camel hair coat and a brimmed hat," Little said, referring to Syracuse star Ernie Davis. "There he was, the first African American to win the Heisman Trophy. My sisters were overwhelmed. They fell in love with him. He was very soft-spoken, very handsome, very articulate. There was just something about him. He had a presence." By the time that evening ended, Little told Davis he was coming to Syracuse.

I wasn't totally committed. I'd known Ernie only a few hours, but he had touched me so much. My family felt if Syracuse could produce a gentleman like him, it must be a good place.

Never once did Ernie tell me, you should go to Syracuse. He did tell me about his experiences at the school and about how he and other black students had been treated by professors and coaches and other students. I appreciated his honesty. I didn't feel like he was trying to sell me on anything. He showed concern for me and gave me useful information and left the decision to me.

Little kept his verbal commitment to Davis a secret and recruiters continued to pursue him, but on the spring day in 1963 when Davis died of leukemia, Little knew exactly where he was going. "I was at Bordentown when one of my teammates came up and told me something I couldn't believe," he said. "I listened to the radio to see if it was true. Then, I heard it, 'Ernie Davis, Syracuse great, Heisman Trophy winner, first player taken in the draft,' had died of leukemia before playing a down in the NFL. I picked up the phone and told coach Schwartzwalder I was coming to Syracuse."

His performance as a sophomore against Kansas was a harbinger of things to come as he would go on to break virtually every record Brown and Davis had established. He'd also go on to become the first Syracuse football player since Joe Alexander (1918–1920) to earn All-American honors three consecutive seasons, and some were convinced that Little would have gone four-for-four had he not played during an era when freshmen weren't eligible to play varsity football.

After leading the freshman team in rushing, scoring, and pass receiving, Little moved up to the varsity and broke Davis's sophomore rushing record and led the Orangemen in scoring, pass receiving, and punt and kickoff returns. His all-purpose yardage total was 1,686 yards.

Little became the first Syracuse back in history to surpass 1,000 yards in a season in 1965 (1,065), he led the nation in all-purpose yardage with 1,990, and his 19 touchdowns and 114 points remain SU standards.

He then completed his collegiate career by rushing for 811 yards and scoring 15 touchdowns as a senior, giving him a school record total of 46, a mark he held alone until Walter Reyes tied it in 2004. In 1966, Little finished fifth in the Heisman Trophy voting and might have won the award had voters not been required to cast their ballots before bowl games. Teaming with fullback Larry Csonka, he saved his best for last,

A familiar sight on Saturday afternoons at Archbold during the 1965 and '66 seasons—fullback Larry Csonka leading the way for halfback Floyd Little. The two formed one of the most dynamic one-two punches in college football history.

rushing for 216 yards in an 18-12 loss to Tennessee in the 1966 Gator Bowl.

Little spent eight seasons in the NFL, and although he didn't have the success at the pro level that he enjoyed in college, he was the player who helped establish the Denver Broncos as one of the league's most successful franchises. Despite playing with a weak supporting cast, Little rushed for 6,323 yards and

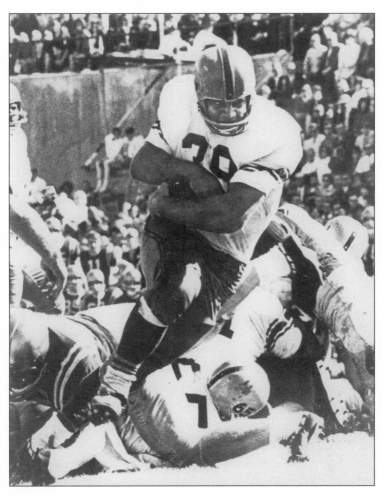

Larry Csonka became the first Syracuse running back to amass two
1,000-yard seasons, topping the plateau in both 1966 and '67.

*43 touchdowns and earned four Pro Bowl invitations. His best season was
1971 when he led the league in rushing with 1,133 yards. In 1984, he became
the first player inducted into the Broncos' Ring of Fame. Following his playing career, he earned his law degree and became a successful businessman in the
automotive industry. He has received numerous awards for his service to his
community.*

Orange Slice—Jim Nance

He is usually overlooked when the discussion turns to great Syracuse University running backs, and that's too bad because Jim Nance made a huge impact on the Hill in the early 1960s. Just ask any defender who attempted to get in his way.

At six-feet, 240 pounds, Nance packed quite a wallop, whether carrying the ball or clearing a path for others. He would begin the tradition of bruising Orange fullbacks that would be carried on by the likes of Larry Csonka, Daryl Johnston, and Rob Konrad.

Nance was exceptionally quick and nimble for his size. He ran the 100-yard dash in 10.1 seconds, and the agility and leverage he displayed on the wrestling mat as a two-time NCAA heavyweight champion was evident on the football field, too.

One of ten children fathered by an Indiana, Pennsylvania, coal miner, Nance led the 'Cuse in rushing as a sophomore in 1962 (417 yards) and as a senior in 1964 (951 yards). During his final season with the Orangemen, Nance combined with All-American Floyd Little to form college football's top running-back duo.

He scored 13 touchdowns that year, including at least one in ten straight games, a record that stood until Walter Reyes broke it in 2003, and he helped lead SU to a Sugar Bowl berth in New Orleans against Louisiana State. SU lost the game, 13-10, but Nance had a solid afternoon with 70 yards in just 15 carries.

Selected in the nineteenth round of the American Football League draft by the Boston Patriots, he went on to have an even more productive pro career, finishing with 5,401 yards and 45 touchdowns in eight seasons. Twice, he led the AFL in rushing and was the league's most valuable player in 1966 when he set AFL single-season records for carries (299) and yards (1,458).

Asked what it was like to tackle Nance, Houston Oilers linebacker Ronnie Caveness responded: "He hit me so hard that my whole family felt it."

After an ankle injury ruined his 1968 season, Nance gained 750 yards in 1969 and was named the AFL's Comeback Player of the Year, but he never regained his form, and he played out his career with the Patriots, New York Jets, and Memphis of the World Football League.

Tragedy dogged Nance after he retired from football in 1974. On back-to-back days in 1983 he suffered a heart attack and a stroke. In 1991 his daughter Nicole was severely injured in a car accident, and she later died from her injuries. And on June 16, 1992, at the age of forty-nine, Nance died of a heart attack.

Jim Nance

Date of birth: December 30, 1942

Hometown: Indiana, Pennsylvania

Honors: Honorable mention All-America in 1964. . . . Voted SU's team MVP in 1964. . . . Selected to play in Coaches All-American All-Star Game in 1965.

Achievements: Led Orange in rushing in 1962 and '64. . . . Won the NCAA heavyweight wrestling championship in 1963 and '65 and was a two-time wrestling All-American.

SU career totals: 325 carries, 1,605 yards, 16 touchdowns.

5

The Ultimate Double-Double

February 8, 1966   *No one in Syracuse basketball history*
Manley Field House   *scored more points in a three-year span*
Syracuse, New York   *than Dave Bing, and the man who put the*
                      Orange basketball program on the map
                      never had a greater night than late in his
                      senior season when he throttled Cornell
                      for thirty-nine points and twenty-five
                      rebounds.

They met for the first time during their freshman year at Syracuse University in a creaky, claustrophobic gymnasium overlooking the spot where the Carrier Dome now stands.

A pickup basketball game was played, and Jim Boeheim, a gangly, bespectacled walk-on from a rural town in upstate New York, was assigned to guard Dave Bing, the hotshot recruit from the same Washington, D.C., neighborhood that produced hoops legend Elgin Baylor.

"Dave put on a clinic, beat our team by about 15 points," said Boeheim of the shirts-and-skins scrimmage that occurred four decades ago. "He kicked my butt and I felt bad until I saw him do the same thing to everyone else in America during the next four years. He was some kind of player."

No one appreciates Bing's impact on college hoops and the Syracuse program more than Boeheim, the winningest coach in school history. "The success we continue to enjoy can be traced directly back to Dave Bing," he said. "He's the guy who turned things around here. He raised this program from the ashes."

Fred Lewis, who coached the SU basketball team from 1962 to 1968, convinced Dave Bing to play for the Orangemen, and it was Bing who laid the foundation for the program's future success.

Or, more accurately, from the dust that once accumulated on the old raised wooden basketball court at Manley Field House, Syracuse's hoops home before the Carrier Dome. When Bing and Boeheim arrived as freshmen in the autumn of 1962, football clearly was big man on campus. The Orangemen were still basking in the glow of having won the national football championship three years earlier and were just a year removed from Ernie Davis winning the Heisman Trophy. Football was a source of pride on campus, a symbol of excellence.

Basketball, meanwhile, was a source of ridicule—something students and the local populace followed with lukewarm interest to pass the time from the end of the football season until the annual spring game. "We didn't get any respect," Boeheim said.

> They had just built Manley so the football team would have a place to prepare for bowl games. We were merely an afterthought. They had a dirt floor in Manley, and they placed the basketball court off to the side so we wouldn't get in the way of the football team. They would come in while we were practicing in December, and kick up all this dust. We'd have to stop our practice several times and get dust mops to clean the court off.

While the football team was making an annual bowl appearance, the basketball team was getting bowled over. Two years before Bing joined the varsity, Syracuse lost twenty-seven consecutive games—at the time the longest losing streak in Division I history.

But that would change, thanks to Bing. He would do for Syracuse basketball what Arnold Palmer had done for golf. He would popularize hoops on the hilly campus and help the sport gain equal status with football.

"I think that was part of the appeal of coming to Syracuse," said Bing, founder and CEO of the Bing Group, one of the largest and most successful minority-owned industrial firms in the nation. "Coach [Fred] Lewis convinced me that the Syracuse program had bottomed out and that I could be the catalyst in turning things around. I welcomed that challenge."

Two other factors played a role in Bing's decision to choose the Orangemen over basketball powerhouses UCLA and Maryland. "SU officials were smart enough to schedule my visit in early May, so I had no idea about the way it snows and snows and snows in Syracuse," said Bing, chuckling.

> I'm up there on a sunny, spring day, and the students are all over the place, wearing shorts and having a good old time, and I'm thinking to

myself, "Wow, it must be like this year-round." Nobody told me how bad the winters were.

The other thing that swayed me was Ernie Davis. During my visit I spoke with him at length. What an impressive human being. The way he handled himself on and off the field with such dignity, set a standard, I believe, for everyone at Syracuse to follow. It's such a shame that his life was cut short by leukemia [in the spring of 1963]. I would have loved to have had an opportunity to have gotten to know him better.

In those days, freshmen weren't eligible to play on the varsity. That was unfortunate for Syracuse because Bing and his classmates were vastly more talented than any squad the varsity could put on the floor.

"About four weeks after the start of practice our freshman team scrimmaged the varsity," said Boeheim, who was Bing's backcourt mate for four years and his roommate for two years. "Dave went wild, and we beat them something like 120-60."

In an interview a few years before he died, Lewis recounted that scrimmage, saying: "Word soon spread around campus that we had this fabulous freshman player, and before long we started packing Manley. They would play a freshman game before the varsity game in those days, and everyone would come to see Bing. Then the varsity game would start and half the people would leave. It was embarrassing, but at least we had hope for the future."

In 1963, Bing became eligible to play varsity ball, and his impact was immediate. Syracuse, which only two seasons earlier had won just two of twenty-four games, went 17-8 as Bing averaged 22 points and 12 rebounds per contest. SU slipped to 13-10 his junior season, but the following year the Orangemen went 22-6, led the nation in scoring with a 99-points-per-game average, and reached the NCAA East Regional final, where they lost to Duke, 91-81.

Bing averaged 28.4 points and 10.8 rebounds that season to earn consensus All-American honors. Assist records weren't accurately tabulated in those days, but Boeheim estimates Bing averaged at least 8 per game.

In establishing a single-season school scoring record that still stands, the willowy six-foot-three guard tallied 40 or more points three times during the 1965–1966 campaign, including a 46-point explosion against second-ranked Vanderbilt.

"He was so fluid," Lewis said. "No wasted movement. And his leaping ability and hang time were unbelievable. He could stay in the air all day."

Though not large in stature, Bing remains one of the school's all-time best rebounders. His ability to grab missed shots was never more evident than during the Cornell game in 1966 at Manley. The Orangemen wound up routing a very good Big Red squad, 120-85, that night, and the only true drama was Bing's assault on the SU record book.

During the final five minutes of play, most of the 5,416 spectators were on their feet pleading for Bing's return once word spread that he needed only one more rebound to surpass the modern Syracuse single-game record.

Lewis wound up heeding their request, and Bing grabbed three more boards to finish with twenty-five. He also scored thirty-nine points in what just might be the best all-around individual performance in SU basketball history.

Lewis was reluctant to put Bing back in the game because he didn't want the Cornell coaches, players, and fans to think he was rubbing it in. He finally relented, telling reporters afterward: "It's the shot of a lifetime for a boy. I can't deprive him of the chance. So far the other coaches have been gracious, but how will they treat me when I don't have a Bing?"

After guiding Syracuse to only its second NCAA tournament appearance, Bing was drafted second overall by the NBA's Detroit Pistons in the spring of '66. He earned rookie-of-the-year honors that season and wound up leading the league in scoring in 1968. In 1981, Syracuse retired his number 22 jersey, and nine years later Bing was inducted into the Naismith Basketball Hall of Fame in Springfield, Massachusetts. When the NBA celebrated its fiftieth anniversary, Bing was named one of the league's fifty greatest players of all time.

Orange Slice—Jim Boeheim

Colgate University was interested in him, and his basketball coach at Lyons Central High School in rural upstate New York urged him to go there. But Jim Boeheim wanted to play basketball at a higher level in college. So the skinny teenager showed up at Syracuse University in the

Dave Bing drives for a layup as his teammate and future Syracuse coach, the be-spectacled number 35 Jim Boeheim, gets in position for a potential rebound.

autumn of '62 and attempted to make the Orange hoops team as a non-scholarship walk-on.

Appearances can be deceiving, and that certainly proved to be the case with Boeheim, who entered college carrying just 160 pounds on his six-foot-four frame. Boeheim was an intense competitor with a velvety-soft jumper, razor-sharp elbows, and a coach's intuition and intelligence.

He wound up making the SU varsity in his sophomore year (freshman weren't eligible in those days) and earned a scholarship from SU coach Fred Lewis. During his senior season Boeheim averaged 14.6 points per game while teaming in the backcourt with future Basketball Hall of Famer Dave Bing. The Orangemen led the nation in scoring that season with 99 points per game and made it all the way to the NCAA East Regional, where they lost to Duke.

But Boeheim's greatest impact would be felt as a coach. Named to replace Roy Danforth in 1976, he guided the Orangemen to twenty-three NCAA tournament appearances and twenty-seven twenty-victory seasons in his first twenty-nine years on the job. And he reached the apex of his coaching career when the 'Cuse won the NCAA basketball championship in 2003 behind the exploits of precocious freshmen Carmelo Anthony and Gerry McNamara.

For many years, Boeheim was underappreciated by fans, media, and some members of the coaching fraternity. After more than seven hundred victories, that's not an issue anymore.

"When I think of Syracuse basketball, two words come immediately to mind—Jim Boeheim," said Dick Vitale, the longtime ESPN college basketball commentator. "The 'Cuse and Boeheim are inseparable. They go together perfectly like spaghetti and meatballs." Added John Thompson, a longtime Boeheim nemesis while coaching at Georgetown: "He's created a program that year-in and year-out demands excellence, and that's not easy to sustain in the dog-eat-dog world of college basketball. Most programs hit a rut at some point, and it's tough for them to get out of it. Jim's program has never been in a rut for any prolonged period of time, and that's a tribute to him."

Boeheim, the winningest coach in school history, received numerous offers to leave his alma mater through the years—some of them quite lucrative from other colleges and a handful of NBA teams. But he decided long ago to be true to his school and establish Syracuse as one of the premier basketball programs of all time. "Some people are meant to be where they are, and that's it," he said.

He essentially showed up on campus in 1962 and never left—spending time as a student, assistant coach, and head coach. Good thing for him and SU hoops that he didn't take that advice and head off to Colgate so many years ago.

Jim Boeheim

Date of birth: November 17, 1944

Hometown: Lyons, New York

Honors: Inducted into the Naismith Basketball Hall of Fame on September 9, 2005. . . . Member of SU All-Century Team. . . . Three-time Big East Coach of the Year. . . . Earned SU Letterman of Distinction honor in 1988. . . . Carrier Dome court was renamed Jim Boeheim Court in 2000. . . . Claire Bee Award winner in 2000. . . . Presented SU's most prestigious alumni award, the Arents Award, in 2000. . . . Member of the Greater Syracuse Sports Hall of Fame.

Achievements: Is winningest coach in SU history as well as all-time leader in Big East Conference victories. . . . Has led Orange to NCAA Tournament in twenty-four of twenty-nine seasons, and his teams have won at least twenty games in twenty-seven seasons. . . . Surpassed 700-win plateau in 2005, and he ranks nineteenth on the all-time Division I victory list through 2005. . . . Seven of his former assistants are Division I head coaches, including Rick Pitino.

SU career totals: Coaching record of 703-241. . . . As a player he had 745 points and 177 rebounds.

6

Roy's Runts Reincarnated

March 20, 1975
Providence Civic Center
Providence, Rhode Island

No one gave the Orangemen much of a chance in their NCAA Tournament East Regional semifinal against Dean Smith's North Carolina Tar Heels, but Jimmy Lee's jumper with five seconds left produced a shocking upset and paved the road to Syracuse's first trip to the Final Four.

It was the day before Syracuse was to play mighty North Carolina in the semifinals of the 1975 NCAA Tournament's East Regional, and shooting guard Jimmy Lee wasn't sure he and the Orangemen were in the right place. "I remember we were up there and everyone was saying the winner of the Kansas State–Boston College game was going to play North Carolina in the finals," Lee recalled. "We were like 'Wait a minute, are we here?'"

Yes, Roy Danforth's Orangemen, ranked twentieth in the latest Associated Press poll, were in Providence. They were the fourth team in the East Regional bracket, the other team, the team that everyone figured was there only to play the role of punching bag for Dean Smith's sixth-ranked, star-studded, and supposedly superior Tar Heels. "Nobody gave us a chance, we had nothing to lose, nobody expected us to do anything," Lee continued. "Everyone expected us to get beat so we were going to go out and have fun and play our game. That was our feeling. We thought we could win the game, but we might have been the only ones who thought that."

The following night, the Orangemen were not alone. Trailing 76-75

42

Jimmy Lee was a sweet-shooting guard who, during the run to the Final Four in 1975, hit one of the biggest shots in Syracuse history, a last-second jumper that lifted Syracuse over North Carolina in the East Regional semifinal.

with the clock withering down to single ticks, Lee took a kick-out pass from Rudy Hackett to the left of the key about twenty feet from the basket and let fly with a jumper that became not only the biggest of his splendid Syracuse career but also one of the most important in Orange basketball history.

The ball splashed through the net with five seconds remaining, and when the Tar Heels botched the ensuing inbounds play and fouled Syracuse point guard Jimmy Williams, the "Bug" sank one free throw to complete the shocking 78-76 conquest of North Carolina. "We were given no shot, and they might have won nine of the next 10 games if we had played, but that one game, we won," said Lee, who poured in 24 points on 12-for-18 shooting from the floor.

Lee grew up on the New York–Pennsylvania border in Kirkwood, and Syracuse may have well have been Siberia. "Last exit on route 81 before you get into Pennsylvania," he said. "I hardly even knew where Syracuse was until Mike came up here to play."

Mike was Lee's older brother, who preceded him in Manley Field House by two years. Mike and Jimmy Lee formed a talented tandem in high school in Kirkwood, and after Mike earned a scholarship to Syracuse, Jim concluded that he wanted to do the same thing. "I liked playing ball with Mike, he was a great team player and we had played good together in high school," said Lee, who still resides in Syracuse and now goes by the more adultlike name Jim. "I enjoyed playing with Mike. I was his little brother for a little while [at Syracuse], but in the end I did OK for myself. And he helped me a lot with little comments here or there."

The brothers played only one season together (1972–1973) because freshmen weren't eligible for the varsity in those days, but Mike, then a senior, played a huge role in Jim's development as a player. "In my sophomore year when I got playing time, he'd tell me, 'Hey Jim, they didn't put you in to rebound or play defense. Shoot the ball or coach is going to take you out,' " Jim said. "I enjoyed playing with Mike. We got along good and he was kind of my hero anyway, so it worked out great."

That year Jim averaged 8.9 points per game off the bench and helped the Orangemen advance to the NCAA Tournament for the first time since 1966 when Fred Lewis coached a team that was led by seniors Dave Bing and Jim Boeheim. Syracuse lost in the East Regional semifinals to Maryland.

Once players like Mike Lee, Dennis Duval, and Mark Wadach graduated, Jim Lee, Hackett, Williams, and Chris Sease took the baton and guided the Orangemen to another NCAA berth in 1974, though they fell in the first round to Oral Roberts.

Coming into 1975, expectations were high on the Hill. Lee and Hackett were seniors who provided excellent leadership, not to mention about 38 points per game; Sease was an explosive player on the break, and he could knock down jumpers; Williams was a speedy and creative point guard; and Kevin King, Earnie Seibert, and Bob Parker could get physical on the glass.

The Orangemen won eleven of their first thirteen games, then hit a lull and lost five of eight before getting their act together down the stretch. They won four in a row to close the regular season at 18-7, drubbed Niagara and St. Bonaventure in the Eastern Collegiate Athletic Conference (ECAC) playoffs to earn their berth into the NCAAs, then survived an 87-83 overtime thriller in the first round against LaSalle, a game played on LaSalle's home floor, the Palestra. "They gave us a second life when Joe Bryant [Kobe Bryant's father] missed a baseline jumper at the end of regulation, and then we went on and beat them in overtime to get to the regionals," said Lee.

Up next were the Tar Heels, a team composed of future NBA players Phil Ford, Tommy LaGarde, Walter Davis, and Mitch Kupchak, and although North Carolina was painted as a prohibitive favorite, there was at least one man who didn't bleed orange who was wary of Syracuse. "We know Syracuse is a hell of a team," said Dean Smith. "I think Roy has done a great job coaching that team, especially the way he's got them running the fast break. I think it's going to be a hell of a game."

It was, mainly because the Orangemen were completely confident in their ability not only to compete but to win as well. Never mind that North Carolina had won the ACC Tournament by taking down defending national champion North Carolina State in the final, then crushed New Mexico State by twenty-four points in the opening round of the NCAAs. "I think we've got a good shot at North Carolina," Danforth said. "They've got a hell of a club, but so do we. Sometimes you can be a little awed of a team from a conference with the ACC's reputation, but our players aren't going to be awed by North Carolina. That's not going to be a problem."

That's what riding a seven-game winning streak will do for a team, said Lee. "We had just started to peak," he said. "We only lost seven games all year [heading into the game], but as I think back most of those were close games that could have gone either way. We had a quiet confidence about us because we were starting to play good."

North Carolina charged at the start and opened a 6-0 lead, then stretched its advantage to nine points on a couple of occasions. The duo of LaGarde and Kupchak effectively took Hackett—SU's leading scorer with a 22.6 average—out of the game, denying him the ball on every Syracuse possession. Then Hackett got into foul trouble and sat down for the final six minutes of the half with three personals.

However, with Lee and Williams draining outside shots, the Orangemen fought back, and an eight-point run—accomplished on baskets by King, Lee, Williams, and Sease—tied the game at 40-40. The Tar Heels took a slim 42-41 lead into the locker room.

Hackett had been held scoreless, North Carolina had shot a blistering 67 percent from the floor, yet Syracuse was right there, and Lee remembered thinking, "Once we hung in there in the first half, we knew we could win. I remember the halftime speech that coach Danforth gave, and he said 'We're one point down and Rudy hasn't even scored.' We all thought that was a pretty good point."

Syracuse bolted to its biggest lead of the night, 59-54, but Smith's team—led by the outside bombing of Brad Hoffman who hit ten of twelve shots, all from at least twenty feet—regained the lead and held it until the final seconds.

Ford made a pair of free throws with forty seconds remaining to give the Tar Heels a 76-73 lead, but Syracuse ran downcourt and Sease hit a twenty-foot jumper eight seconds later to cut the Orange deficit to one. Danforth called for a full-court press, and North Carolina threw the ball away, giving Syracuse possession with twenty-seven seconds to go.

It was time for someone to be a hero, and Lee gladly stepped forward. "We had the ball at the side court and we kind of knew what we were going to do, we had practiced for those situations," he said.

> They were in a zone and we were going to work the ball around for the best shot we could get. I got the ball and Rudy was down low so I dumped it down to him and once he had it, I think their whole team thought he was going to shoot it and he had four guys converge on him. He just dumped it back out to me at the foul line extended. Those four guys started running at me, but I was wide open. We all had to find open spots and I happened to be the guy on Rudy's side. I had shot that shot thousands and thousands of times before, so I shot it.

And it went in, bringing a deafening roar from the crowd of nearly eleven thousand that had clearly adopted the underdog Orangemen.

Smith quickly signaled for time-out to set up a desperation play, and when the teams returned to the floor Lee grabbed Parker. "I remember walking Bobby Parker down to the end line because he was going to be the guy guarding the inbounds pass and I just said 'Don't touch any-body, just jump up and down,' " Lee said. "I go back to halfcourt and the next thing you know they run the play and he runs over the guy and he steps on his head, but luckily they threw it out of bounds and there was no call."

Kupchak tried to pass to Mickey Bell, but the ball bounced off his hands and careened out-of-bounds with two seconds to go. Williams was fouled on the ensuing inbounds play, he made the first free throw, missed the second, and when the ball clanged off the rim the clock ran out.

Syracuse was playing in the NCAA Tournament for just the fifth time, and its record to this point was 6-4, so when Danforth beamed, "This has to be the finest hour of Syracuse basketball," no one could argue.

Two days later Hackett atoned for his silent night against North Carolina and scored the tying basket as time expired in the regional final against Kansas State, and Syracuse went on to win 95-87 in overtime to punch its ticket to San Diego. But in the first of their four trips to date to the Final Four, the Orangemen were outclassed by powerhouse Kentucky, 95-79, then lost the consolation game to Louisville in overtime, 96-88. Lee earned a tryout with the San Antonio Spurs of the American Basketball Association, but said, "My size finally caught up with me and I didn't make it." He returned to Syracuse and has never left.

Orange Slice—Rudy Hackett

Sonny Vaccaro, Reebok's senior director of grassroots basketball and one of the most influential men in amateur basketball, knows all about Mount Vernon High School outside New York City. "There must be great water in the city of Mount Vernon," Vaccaro said. "Over the years this community has been as good as anyone. It started with Gus Williams, Scooter McCray and now Ben Gordon. Also, the coaches have been the best. Without hesitation, I think it's one the true hotbeds for high school ball."

You'll have to forgive the sixty-four-year-old Vaccaro, who for years has been running prestigious high school all-star camps and tourna-

Rudy Hackett, here soaring for two points against St. Bonaventure at Buffalo's Memorial Auditorium, ranked number two on Syracuse's all-time rebound list when he graduated.

ments, for forgetting Rudy Hackett, one of the true success stories to come out of the famed Mount Vernon program.

Back in the early 1970s Hackett played football and baseball and ran track for the Knights, but he didn't even bother with basketball because he didn't think he'd ever be able to play for the perennial powerhouse in Westchester County.

When he grew to six-foot-eight between his sophomore and junior years, he decided to give basketball a try. But as he expected, he didn't make the grade, and he—like about 240 other kids that year—was cut from the team. That's when his friend Williams, who would go on to play twelve seasons in the NBA, intervened and pretty much told the coach, "Here's a tall guy. He can jump. All he wants to do is rebound. Let him play."

Williams's speech worked, and after riding the pine as a junior, Hackett became one of the finest players to ever pull on a Mount Vernon jersey. He earned All-American honors as a senior averaging 22.2 points and 12.7 rebounds per game while shooting 58.1 percent from the field. So dominant was Hackett that despite playing just one year on the varsity, he elicited scholarship offers from a variety of schools, ultimately accepting Roy Danforth's plea to come to Syracuse.

Hackett and Jim Lee roomed together for two years, then lived next door to each other their senior year when they helped lead the Orangemen to the Final Four. "Rudy could rebound, shoot the ball, handle the ball, he was a real smart player and he was very team-oriented," said Lee of his classmate who finished his Syracuse career with a 17.2 scoring average and the school's second-highest rebound total of 990, a figure that still ranks fifth even though he played only three seasons. "He got cut his junior year in high school which is hard to believe. He had a great body for playing the game, and off the court he was my kind of guy and that's why we got along so good. You could always count on Rudy. Nothing fancy, but he always ended up with 20 points."

Hackett led the Orangemen in rebounding each of his three years, and his 407 boards as a senior are still the second-best single-season total in Syracuse history behind Derrick Coleman's 422 in 1988–1989.

Rudy Hackett

Date of birth: May 10, 1953

Hometown: Mount Vernon, New York

Honors: Second-team All-America in 1975.

Achievements: When he left SU he was the second-leading rebounder in school history. . . . His 407 rebounds in 1974–1975 remains the second-highest single-season total in school history. . . . Averaged 22.2 points and 12.7 rebounds as a senior.

SU career totals: 1,496 points, 990 rebounds.

7

Oh So Close

October 15, 1977   *The good days were few and far between*
Archbold Stadium   *for Syracuse football during Frank*
Syracuse, New York   *Maloney's coaching tenure, which makes*
it appropriate that one of the highlights
was the thrilling 1977 near miss against
Penn State when Bill Hurley put on an
unforgettable show.

When it was over, Frank Maloney gathered his weary and heart-broken Syracuse Orangemen for a solemn and heartfelt prayer for David Paterno, the son of Penn State football coach Joe Paterno who, on this October 1977 afternoon, was listed in serious condition in a central Pennsylvania hospital with his famous father at his side.

After praying for the recovery of young David, who had suffered a fractured skull in a trampoline mishap the day before, prompting Joe Pa to skip Penn State's trip to Archbold Stadium for its annual eastern showdown with the Orange, Maloney broke down in tears.

He felt bad for the Paterno family, but he felt even worse for his upstart Orangemen. They had given everything they had for the better part of three hours on a gloriously sunny autumn afternoon against their fiercest rival, the tenth-ranked team in the nation, only to fall short by a 31-24 count in what was one of the most entertaining games of an otherwise lost football decade on the Hill.

"Let me say one thing," Maloney said, his eyes still puddled as he met the media. "Joe did the right thing staying with his boy and not

51

Quarterback Bill Hurley and coach Frank Maloney discuss strategy on the side-line. Hurley nearly delivered to Maloney in 1977 what would have been his greatest triumph at Syracuse, but the Orangemen lost a heartbreaker to Penn State.

coming to the game. I know that's where I'd have been under similar conditions. The family comes first."

And then Maloney talked about his extended family, his Orangemen, a team that no one would have believed could have given Penn State—with or without Paterno on the sidelines—such a scare. "God, I love this team. What a super effort."

Maloney was fired following the 1980 season, and for the past twenty-four years he has served as director of ticket sales for the Chicago Cubs. It has been a quarter century since he coached football, but that 1977 Penn State game remains vivid in his memory.

> I do remember that game. It was famous because Joe's son had the accident and he wasn't there, but it was a great game in old Archbold and it was a nose to nose game all the way down to the wire.
>
> The best team I had at Syracuse was the '79 team, but we had a nice ballclub in '77 and Bill Hurley had emerged as a premier quarterback and he had a great game, and I remember our big tight end, Bruce Semall had a great day.
>
> It's funny, this summer [2004] I was out at the Chicago Bears camp one day and I sat down and talked to Matt Suhey for a long time. He played for Penn State at that time and he said he'll never forget that game because it didn't look like anybody was going to stop anybody.

Syracuse football had been in decline for a full decade, since Larry Csonka's final year in 1967. Legendary coach Ben Schwartzwalder's last six teams pieced together a ho-hum record of 29-33-1, including a 2-9 mark in 1973, the worst in his twenty-five years at the helm. Ol' Ben retired after that disappointing season, and his replacement, Maloney, had been trying to get the program back to its once prominent perch atop eastern football. To date he had not been able to do it, as he brought a three-and-a-half-year record of 13-25 into the Penn State game.

And now here came the Nittany Lions, winners of their last six encounters with Syracuse by a cumulative 173-30, a team that would wind up with an 11-1 record in 1977, ranked fifth in the final Associated Press poll.

This remains one of only two games Paterno has missed in his fifty-five-year coaching career, but it certainly didn't look like his team was going to miss him when the game began in typical 1970s Syracuse–Penn

State fashion. Nittany Lion freshman Booker Moore returned the opening kickoff 63 yards to the Syracuse 37, and before five minutes had elapsed Steve Geise scored on a one-yard touchdown run.

If Paterno's absence wasn't the first indication that this wasn't going to be an ordinary day, what happened moments later was. Hurley unfurled a 49-yard pass to Semall, setting Hurley off on a record-breaking day as he set school marks for pass completions (22), attempts (36), yards (329), and total offensive yards (384). The long pass set up a 39-yard Dave Jacobs field goal.

"Hurley was a fantastic quarterback," said Maloney of the player who nearly delivered to him his greatest coaching victory.

> If he had played at Ohio State or Michigan his senior year he would have gotten a lot more exposure and Heisman acclaim.
>
> We recruited him as a running back even though he was a wishbone quarterback at St. Joe's in Buffalo. He played running back his freshman year, then we moved him to quarterback because I always believed as a coach you play with what you've got, don't force anything. If you have unbelievable talent you can force any kind of system on players, but when you don't you have to build around what players can do. His first three or four games they wanted to run him out of town because he was awful, he couldn't hit a pass, couldn't do anything, but you could see he had potential and he developed into a tremendous quarterback.

Penn State made it two possessions, two touchdowns, as Geise plunged into the end zone again, but Syracuse was undeterred and this time responded with a 75-yard touchdown drive in six quick plays. A 36-yard pass to Rich Rosen positioned Syracuse for Semall's 9-yard TD reception on a screen pass, and as he dragged two Penn State defenders across the goal line the 27,029 fans shook the foundation of the old concrete oval.

"We knew State would be hard to run against," Maloney said of Penn State's run defense, which was ranked fourth in the nation. "So we felt we had to pass, and we did. We used automatics at the line and Hurley did great."

But Hurley didn't have as much success in the middle two periods, and during that time Penn State scored 17 straight points to extend its lead to a seemingly insurmountable 31-10.

In so many other games the students could have started heading out to Marshall Street to enjoy the surprisingly warm and sunny autumn day while the alums could have begun their treks back to the suburbs because the Orangemen were toast. Hurley made sure they stayed in their seats, then had them leaping out of them in the fourth quarter.

Late in the third, facing a third-and-18 at his own 16, Hurley threw deep to freshman split end Dave Farneski who caught the ball, then appeared to drop it before tumbling to the ground. The officials dubiously signaled a reception, a call that both benches agreed was horrible, and the Orangemen had a 30-yard gain. Penn State then committed two obvious pass-interference penalties, and Syracuse took advantage when Hurley rolled out and hit Mike Jones with an 11-yard TD pass 13 seconds into the fourth quarter.

The Orange defense halted the Nittany Lions next possession, and Hurley came attacking right back. He hit Art Monk—playing wingback at this stage of his career—for a 39-yard gain to the 7. A couple plays later Bob Avery burrowed over from the 1, and now it was 31-24 with more than 10 minutes still remaining.

Archbold was electric, and the sweet aroma of an upset hung prominently in the air. Another defensive stop of Suhey, Geise, and quarterback Chuck Fusina gave Hurley and the Orangemen a potentially tying possession with 4:42 to go, but now the officials turned their ire toward Syracuse.

Hurley's dazzling 35-yard run put the ball on the Penn State 38, but on the next play center Paul Colvin was nailed for holding. Faced with a third-and-18 dilemma, Hurley connected with Semall for a 40-yard gain to the Penn State 6, but once again, there was yellow laundry on the field. This time tackle Neil Barton was called for holding, and Maloney went ballistic on the sideline as the long gain was nullified. "You can call holding on 100 plays in a game," Maloney said. "Why call it for the first time late in the action when the game is on the line?"

Barton was appalled by the call. "I had the guy walled off," he said. "They weren't putting much pressure on Bill at the time so there was no sense in holding him. When I asked the ref he just said 'You had him.' "

The robbery didn't end there. Following a Syracuse punt, the Orangemen thought they had forced and recovered a fumble by Suhey deep in Penn State territory, but the officials ruled Suhey down on the play. "The whole middle of the line hit him," said linebacker John Kinley, who recovered the apparent fumble. "He was still on his feet when I had the ball. I didn't hear a whistle and I don't think anybody did."

Syracuse ultimately got the ball back with 59 seconds to go and despite all their bad luck continued to press. From the Penn State 35 Hurley dropped back and fired a strike down the middle to Semall, his main man all day. Semall, who had tied the Orange record for receptions in a game with 7, was open, but the ball inexplicably bounced off his hands and fell to the ground as the crowd screamed in agony. "There are no excuses," a teary-eyed Semall said. "I just ran before I had the damn ball." Two plays later Hurley was sacked as the clock ran out, the upset bid dead.

All the gaudy statistics meant nothing to Hurley. "Naturally I'm disgusted," he said. "What we are striving for are victories so it doesn't really matter how close we came to winning."

Syracuse lost to defending national champion Pittsburgh the following week, but it won its last four games of 1977 to finish 6-5. Hurley, who was being touted as a Heisman Trophy candidate in 1978, suffered broken ribs in the opener and missed the rest of the season, and Syracuse fell to 3-8. With Hurley back in 1979 for his senior season and Archbold Stadium in rubble after being knocked down to make room for the Carrier Dome, the Orangemen played all 11 games away from Syracuse, staging "home" games at Buffalo's Rich Stadium, New Jersey's Giants Stadium, and Cornell's Schoellkopf Field. They managed a 6-5 record and earned a trip to the Independence Bowl where they blew out Mc-Neese State in their first postseason game since the 1966 Gator Bowl. Hurley, who played briefly in the NFL as a defensive back, held 22 passing and total offense records when he graduated. He still ranks fourth on Syracuse's all-time total offensive-yardage list with 5,949 yards, and his 384 yards against Penn State remains the third-best single game performance in school history.

Orange Slice—Art Monk

When Art Monk retired from the National Football League following the 1995 season, his 940 receptions were the second most in NFL history, his 12,721 receiving yards the fourth-highest total.

And to think, if not for a decision made by the Syracuse coaching

Before he became one of the NFL's greatest wide receivers, Art Monk spent about half of his Syracuse career playing running back.

staff before the start of the 1979 season, Monk may never have become one of the greatest wide receivers in NFL history. "He played multiple positions in high school, and he was a state hurdles champion, so when we recruited him we knew we were getting a great athlete," said Orange coach Frank Maloney. "We weren't sure where we were going to play him. Art was a big boy, tall and thin, and you didn't know if he'd develop into a 240-pound guy because he had a big frame on him when he came in."

When Monk arrived from White Plains, Maloney first used him as a wingback, and he became a dual threat as a runner and receiver. He rushed for 566 yards, second only to quarterback Bill Hurley's 625, and he led the team with 41 catches for 590 yards, 188 of those yards coming in one game against Navy when he caught a still-standing school record 14 balls.

But in 1978, when Hurley suffered a season-ending injury in the opener against Florida State, there wasn't much need for a prolific receiver, so Maloney, on the advice of his offensive coordinator, current New York Giants head coach Tom Coughlin, switched Monk to running back so the Orangemen could more easily get him the ball.

That was the year freshman Joe Morris burst on the scene, and he and Monk shared the backfield, with Morris carrying 170 times for 1,001 yards, Monk 136 times for 573 yards. Monk led the nonexistent pass attack with 19 receptions for 273 yards.

"He was the best athlete we had and we felt like we had to have someone who could run the football, and he was pretty good back there," said Maloney. "Not great, but pretty good. But with Morris in there, in '79 we put Art back to what we felt was his normal position, wideout, and he's been better than I or anybody ever dreamed he would be."

The easygoing Monk gladly accepted the switch back, and as a senior he led the Orangemen for the third year in a row in receptions, with 40 for a career-best 716 yards, giving him a then school record 102 career catches. When he left Syracuse, he had 1,150 rushing yards, 1,644 in receiving and 1,105 in returns, for an all-purpose total of 3,899, second only to Floyd Little at the time and still fourth best.

"With most receivers, you can study film to get the idiosyncrasies in their movements," said Warren Harvey, an SU defensive back who was Monk's best friend and roommate during their days together on the Hill. "He gave away no tell-tale signs. He was so nice and smooth, so fluid, you couldn't tell he ran that fast. Once he got up on you, it was a little too late. He had incredible hands, good concentration."

Monk's pass-catching prowess caught the attention of the Washington Redskins who chose him in the first round of the 1980 draft, eighteenth overall. It wasn't long before he began to craft one of the great careers in league history, a career that has curiously been overlooked thus far by the Pro Football Hall of Fame electorate.

"We had four or five guys who went on to play in the NFL, but he was head and shoulders above everybody else," said Rich Solomon, currently the defensive backs coach for the Arizona Cardinals who was Syracuse's receivers coach in 1979.

After helping the Redskins win Super Bowl XVII, Monk led the NFL with a then record 106 catches in 1984, which began a string of three consecutive Pro Bowl seasons. He also helped the Redskins win Super

Bowls XXII and XXVI, and in that last championship game against Buffalo he had seven receptions for 113 yards. "Quiet about his work, very loud with his results," former Redskins quarterback Mark Rypien once said.

Art Monk

Date of birth: December 5, 1957

Hometown: White Plains, New York

Honors: All-American in 1979. . . . Member of SU's All-Century Team.

Achievements: When he left SU he held a school record with 102 receptions, and he ranked second only to Floyd Little in all-purpose yardage with 3,899. . . . Still holds record for most catches in a game, with 14. . . . Went on to play sixteen seasons in NFL, catching 940 passes for 12,721 yards and playing on three Super Bowl–winning teams with the Washington Redskins.

SU career totals: 102 receptions for 1,644 yards, 1,150 rushing yards, 1,105 return yards.

A Forgettable Farewell

February 13, 1980
Manley Field House
Syracuse, New York

The heated Syracuse-Georgetown basket-ball rivalry was born a quarter century ago when the Hoyas upset the Orangemen in the final game played at Manley Field House, ending Syracuse's fifty-seven-game home-court winning streak and, as John Thompson said, "officially closed" the Zoo.

I t was the basketball pits, replete with uncomfortable metal bleachers and a warped, pieced-together wooden court that rose above a dirt floor. The lighting was terrible. There was even an odor to the place. Smelled kind of like an attic in the heat of the summer.

Dumpiness notwithstanding, there was a certain charm to Manley Field House, Syracuse University's basketball home before the Carrier Dome. It had character and characters. There was a reason it became known affectionately and derisively—depending on your allegiances—as the Zoo.

Originally constructed in 1962 as a place where Syracuse's nationally ranked football team could practice during inclement weather, Manley eventually became famous and infamous for its rowdy basketball ambience. During the 1970s, it became one of the toughest courts in the United States for visiting teams to play. From 1971 through 1980, when SU hoops moved to the Dome, the Orangemen recorded a 121-6 record at Manley that included winning streaks of 36 and 57 games.

The cozy confines of Manley Field House gave the Orangemen a huge home-court advantage, and thanks to the denizens of the Zoo, Syracuse reeled off winning streaks of thirty-six and fifty-seven games in the building.

With a seating capacity of just over 9,200, fans sat so close to the action they could count a player's nose hairs. Proximity clearly bred fear. There were numerous occasions when opposing players and referees were intimidated by the raucous spectators. "At Manley, you had fans so close to the floor they could literally touch the players and officials," said Roosevelt Bouie, a former All-American center at Syracuse. "The Dome is a spacious country club by comparison."

In Bouie's four seasons as a varsity starter, the Orange went 55-1 at home. "It was a pride thing with us," he said. "We didn't want anybody coming into our house and leaving with a smile. We wanted it to be a House of Horrors for them, and we felt we had the best sixth man advantage in the country because our student cheering section was absolutely wild. They'd be getting on the other team the minute they got off the bus."

Nearly a quarter century has passed since the six-foot-eleven Bouie swatted away his last shot at Manley. And, despite the passage of time, it still gnaws at him that he and his teammates didn't finish their careers with a perfect home record.

The only blemish on their otherwise spotless ledger was dealt to them by Georgetown, and not only did the 52-50 Hoyas victory snap SU's school-record fifty-seven-game home winning streak, it ignited a rivalry between the two schools that would become as fierce as any in college basketball.

The Orangemen entered that game ranked number two in the country with a 21-1 record and were heavily favored to extend their streak against the 17-5 Hoyas. SU sprinted to a 28-14 lead with four minutes remaining in the first half, and coach Jim Boeheim instructed his team to slow the pace down and begin milking the clock.

The strategy worked for a while as, much to the delight of the 9,251 spectators, the Orangemen extended their lead to 16 points in the second half. But thanks to some hot shooting by the Hoyas and some poor shooting by Syracuse, Georgetown gradually reduced the deficit, setting up a nail-biting finish. The visitors began fouling SU players in the final minutes in hopes of stopping the clock, and the Orangemen failed to capitalize on the strategy, converting just one of eight free throws.

With five seconds remaining and the game tied at 50, Hoyas sophomore guard Eric "Sleepy" Floyd calmly hit two free throws to give Georgetown its first lead of the night. The ball was inbounded quickly and passed to Louis Orr who missed a thirty-foot shot at the buzzer. For the first time in nearly four years, the Orangemen walked off their court in defeat.

"We were really bummed because that was the last game in Manley—they were moving the games to the Dome the following season—and we wanted so badly to close the place with a win," Bouie said. "It was a real downer."

In his postgame press conference, Georgetown coach John Thompson opted not to leave town quietly. Rubbing salt in the wound, Thompson announced bombastically: "Manley Field House is officially closed." After uttering those incendiary words, Thompson went from being an anonymous coach to basketball enemy number one in the eyes of the Orange faithful.

"Coach Boeheim was disappointed and we were, too," Bouie recalled. "They came into town and ruined our party. And then when Coach Thompson made that statement that just got people even more riled. From that point on, whenever he and his team came to town, the crowds really got on him. He became Big, Bad John, the guy they loved to hate."

Thompson, a huge presence at six-foot-ten, recognized the rivalry as great theater, the hoops equivalent of Yankees–Red Sox. He fed off the hostile fans, and they off him. He often raised the noise level several decibels by smiling at the booing throng or by waving his signature towel above his head.

Thompson also knew how to raise the blood-pressure level of his coaching counterpart. "In the early years, those games started out very warlike," Boeheim recalled. "The intensity among our players and fans was incredible. We wanted to beat their brains in, and they wanted to do the same to us. I've talked to several refs who've worked a number of Final Fours, and they said those Syracuse-Georgetown games were much tougher to work because of the emotions among the players, coaches and fans. They came away from those nights totally exhausted. All of us did."

Boeheim and Thompson eventually became good friends. But their competitiveness was so intense in the 1980s that there was at least one occasion when they almost went toe-to-toe. "I wasn't going to fight him; I wasn't that stupid," said Boeheim, who was giving up six inches and nearly one hundred pounds to Big John. "But I was fighting angry, and so was he. In later years, he mellowed and so did I, and we were able to joke about things. But in the beginning there was nothing funny when these two teams took the floor."

Throughout much of the 1980s and '90s, the SU-Georgetown game was the hottest ticket in Syracuse, with the Hoyas' annual visit often attracting crowds in excess of thirty thousand. "There were a lot of people who had moved from Syracuse to Florida who would fly back just for that game," Boeheim said. "That's what an attraction it was."

And its roots can be traced to SU's home before the Dome and six inflammatory words uttered by a visiting coach who would become the main villain in one of college basketball's most compelling passion plays.

Manley Field House was officially reopened for men's basketball business on November 16, 1994. With the football team occupying the Carrier Dome, the Orange hoopsters played a preseason National Invitational Tournament game in Manley, and visiting George Washington University was hardly a gracious guest. The Colonials wound up upsetting SU, 111-104, in overtime, almost fifteen years after Thompson's Georgetown team wrecked the party and the Orange home-court winning streak.

Orange Slice—The Louie and Bouie Show

One was a six-foot-eleven center from a rural one-traffic-light town on the shores of Lake Ontario in Upstate New York. The other was a pencil-thin six-foot-eight forward from a big high school in Cincinnati. Together, Roosevelt Bouie and Louis Orr would get Jim Boeheim's coaching career at Syracuse off to a flying start.

In their four years as varsity starters—a hoops era known fondly at SU as "The Louie and Bouie Show"—the Orangemen went 100-18 and earned four NCAA Tournament appearances. "They were the two that got the ball rolling for us in the late 1970s," Boeheim said. "As far as my head-coaching career, it all goes back to them. They helped me get off to a great beginning."

Bouie, the New York State Scholastic Player of the Year at Kendall High School in 1976, was the first big-name recruit Boeheim landed. "We were in a dog-fight with St. Bonaventure for Rosie, and I'm so glad we got him because he gave us instant credibility," Boeheim said. "He was a big, intimidating, shot-blocking center. He made everybody better, particularly on defense, because he was quite a presence in the middle. If you got past one of our defenders, you'd still have to face Rosie and that was like driving against a brick wall."

No one would have described Orr as a brick wall. But his skinny physique belied superb skills as a scorer and rebounder. "I think his body actually worked to his advantage," Bouie said. "People looked at him and thought they were going to have an easy night. They quickly discovered that appearances can be deceiving."

How Orr wound up at Syracuse is the stuff of legend. At Boeheim's urging, SU assistant Rick Pitino delayed his honeymoon and went to Cincinnati to stake out Orr. Pitino, who would go on to become a highly successful coach at Kentucky and Louisville, eventually convinced Orr to accept the scholarship offer.

By the time their careers on the Hill were finished, they were two of

Louis Orr (55) and Roosevelt Bouie (50) were part of the first recruiting class of Jim Boeheim, and they went on to become two
of the finest players to wear the Syracuse uniform.

Syracuse's all-time greats, Bouie ranking second in points behind only
Dave Bing with 1,560, and Orr at number six with 1,487. Bouie still is
number two on the blocked-shots list with 327 behind only Etan
Thomas.

Bouie wound up being chosen in the second round of the 1980 NBA
draft by the Dallas Mavericks but turned down their contract offer when
the team wouldn't guarantee its $65,000 salary offer. He headed for the
Italian League in Europe and was presented an offer he could not refuse:
a guaranteed $100,000 contract, a Mercedes, and a three-bedroom, two-
balcony flat on the shores of the Adriatic Sea. It was, Bouie said at the
time, "a choice between a secure job and an insecure job."

He never played in the NBA but spent twelve years in Italy and one in Spain and became one of the most successful American players to play overseas, a pioneer of sorts.

"What people don't know is that my dream growing up was to be a successful businessman," he said. "I wanted to get up, go to work all dressed up and everything I touched would turn to gold. It just so happened I also loved basketball." Today, Bouie is living that dream as a multimillionaire who is involved in a number of business ventures.

Orr was drafted five slots above his old running mate in the second round of that draft by Indiana and spent eight successful seasons as a forward in the NBA with the Pacers and New York Knicks. Orr returned to Syracuse to serve on Boeheim's staff for several seasons before taking over as the head coach at Siena College and later one of SU's Big East rivals, Seton Hall.

Roosevelt Bouie

Date of birth: January 21, 1958

Hometown: Kendall, New York

Honors: Member of SU All-Century Team. . . . Honorable mention All-America in 1979 and '80. . . . First-team All–Big East in 1980.

Achievements: Owns SU NCAA Tournament record for blocked shots in a game with 8. . . . Had 38 career double-doubles, seventh best in SU history. . . . Ranks second all time in blocked shots with 327 and led team all four years he played. . . . Career field-goal percentage of .593 is third best in school history, and his .654 mark in 1979–1980 is a school record.

SU career totals: 1,560 points, 987 rebounds, 327 blocked shots.

Louis Orr

Date of birth: May 7, 1958

Hometown: Cincinnati, Ohio

Honors: Member of SU All-Century Team. . . . Honorable mention All-America in 1980. . . . First-team All–Big East in 1980. . . . Presented Vic Hanson Medal of Excellence award in 1990.

Achievements: Is now the head coach at SU rival Seton Hall and was 2003 Big East Coach of the Year. . . . Played in the NBA with the Indiana Pacers and New York Knicks. . . . Was also an assistant at Syracuse, Providence, and Xavier and head coach at Siena before taking Seton Hall job in 2001. . . . Had 27 career double-doubles, ninth best in SU history.

SU career totals: 1,487 points, 881 rebounds.

9

Dome Sweet Dome

September 20, 1980   *One of the most exciting nights in the uni-*
Carrier Dome   *versity's history, not to mention the city of*
Syracuse, New York   *Syracuse's history, was the opening of the*
Carrier Dome, and the spectacular venue
was christened properly by Joe Morris who
led Syracuse to victory over Miami of
Ohio.

Nearly thirty years have passed since Bobby Bowden last took his West Virginia Mountaineers to Syracuse to play the Orangemen at ancient Archbold Stadium, and the memory of that day apparently remains permanently implanted in Bowden's mind.

In the week leading up to Florida State's visit to the Carrier Dome in October 2004, the legendary Seminoles coach harkened back to 1975 when his nationally ranked team suffered a shocking 20-19 loss to Frank Maloney's Orangemen—"He wasn't then what he is now," Maloney quipped of Bowden—on a typically raw and sloppy November Syracuse afternoon. "I like playing in the Carrier Dome if we're going to go that far north," Bowden said. "When I was at West Virginia we played Syracuse every year, and there ain't nothing worse than playing in old Archbold. At least I know we ain't gonna see rain, cold or snow out there. If it's cold now, they can just turn the thermostat up."

Never was that thermostat hotter than the September night twenty-five years ago when the Carrier Dome opened its revolving, pressurized doors right on the very land where once proud and stately—but later rat-infested and decrepit—Archbold stood.

Dave Warner (11), Jim Collins (33), and Joe Morris (47) await the opening coin toss before the inaugural game at the Carrier Dome on September 20, 1980.

The temperature was comfortably warm outside that night in 1980, but it was positively saunalike inside the non-air-conditioned Dome when Maloney's seventh and final Orange football team christened the sparkling new athletic palace—the only one of its kind on a college campus—with a 36-24 victory over Miami of Ohio. "I do remember that it was very warm inside the building," Maloney said, recalling the irony of Syracuse-based air-conditioning giant Carrier Corporation buying the naming rights to a stadium that did not have air-conditioning.

Many of the folks who today attend events in what is still the only domed stadium in the Northeast never braved the elements for a game at old Archbold. But those who sat on the steel bleachers or, even worse, the cold, hard concrete will never forget the Archbold experience. For example, the 2004 Syracuse Football Season Ticket Holders of the Year, Jack and Joan Casey of Fayetteville. The couple, married more than fifty years and Orange supporters since their teenage days, were interviewed by Dick Case of the Syracuse *Post-Standard,* and Joan, a former

SU student and later an employee in the admissions office, said, "Oh, the times we had in Archbold."

And undeniably, there were great times in the days when the Saltine Warrior roamed the sidelines, Bill Orange paraded around on stilts, the ATO touchdown cannon celebrated scoring plays, pretty Dottie Grover twirled her baton, placard cheering was all the rage, and football heroes such as Vic Hanson, Lew Andreas, Roy Simmons Sr., Jim Brown, Gerhard Schwedes, Roger Davis, Jim Ringo, Ernie Davis, John Mackey, Floyd Little, Jim Nance, Larry Csonka, Tommy Myers, Art Monk, Joe Morris, and Bill Hurley thrilled the masses.

At the time of its construction in 1907, Archbold was designated as the "Greatest Athletic Arena in America," and the architects made the claim that the building—designed to resemble the Roman Coliseum—would never become outdated.

But as early as the 1940s the massive concrete bowl had begun to show signs of aging, and there was talk of building a new stadium on the site where Manley Field House now sits. Lack of finances killed that plan, and Archbold continued to grow old. In 1968 there was a trial balloon sent up calling for a fifty thousand–seat open-air stadium at the state fairgrounds. Again, the plan was quashed.

Meanwhile, the once formidable football program led by coach Ben Schwartzwalder was suffering. With a crumbling stadium and a lack of other amenities, ol' Ben struggled to bring in quality players, and the Orangemen became perennial losers in his last few years. "We had a budget of $25,000 for recruiting; I couldn't even give our coaches mileage," Schwartzwalder recalled shortly after his 1973 retirement. "And in those days it was legal to give a kid up to $25 a month for laundry and things like that. We didn't even do that."

When Maloney took over in 1974, he had serious doubts about the program's viability.

> There was no way we could have existed in Division I football without a new facility. We had arguably the worst stadium in the country. Anytime a recruit came to town, we never took him to the stadium which is fundamental; you always take a recruit to the stadium. Getting the Dome built was immensely huge for Syracuse to be a contender in the future. It was something they had to do. I think football would have seen its demise there without it.

As it always is, money was the central stumbling block. The Athletic Department had little, and the city, county, and state seemed none too interested in footing the bill.

> There was a lot of in-fighting. It all came down to who was going to fund it, which is the case with all stadiums today. The best I can remember is they had a price tag on what it would cost and the university either didn't have that money or was unwilling to give that much, so they tried to get involved politically with the state. There was a couple of years of wrangling over who was going to pay for it.
>
> And there was also an element that I remember in town of whether we wanted to be Division I. Did we want to move in another direction with football? Do we want to be more like an Ivy League school? It was a smaller segment, but it was out there. There was a debate with where they wanted to go in football.

A feasibility study was conducted in 1976, and it was determined that a fifty thousand–seat stadium could be built in the Syracuse suburb of Salina for between $12 million and $15 million, but the town protested vehemently, and the legislature passed a resolution declaring the county-owned tract was unavailable for stadium purposes.

The Metropolitan Development Association, which had begun the push for a new stadium, put together the Municipal Stadium Commission to solve the problem, and after dozens of sites were considered and rejected, Chancellor Melvin Eggers, in July 1978, proposed the idea of a $35 million domed stadium, student union, and continuing education center on the Archbold site.

New York governor Hugh Carey pledged his support, and more than $15 million in state money was awarded. The university undertook its most ambitious fund-raising push, and Carrier Corporation pitched in $2.75 million in exchange for placing its name on the building.

That just about covered the cost of the $26.85 million project, and moments after the Orangemen upset Navy on November 11, 1978, the fans began demolishing Archbold themselves, tearing out seats and chunks of sod from the field and ripping down railings and the goalposts.

> I don't know how much excitement there was on campus, but internally, within the football program, we had excitement because we were the

ones who had to go out and recruit, go in the homes, and at least you had something to sell now.

We had such a bad image from so many factors the previous 10 years. There was the racial problem [in 1970], the old stadium, and it just seemed like no one cared about football. We'd go into a home and show pictures of what it was going to look like. And the weather was always a huge factor against us in recruiting, so now that was another thing where we could say, "Hey, weather is no longer a problem."

On opening night Maloney came up with an exciting way to open the Dome era: He had kicker Gary Anderson try a daring onside kick. It didn't work, as Anderson kicked the ball out-of-bounds, and with great field position at midfield, Miami marched right down and scored a touchdown, quieting the crowd of 50,564, still the largest gathering in Dome history. "The reason we did that is we had studied a lot of Miami film and we thought we could pull it off," said Maloney. "We didn't pull it off and that was an immediate downer. Miami scored a touchdown after that, but then Joe Morris just took over. It was all Joe Morris that night."

For the record, the first touchdown in Dome history was a six-yard pass from Chuck Hauck to Greg Jones, but Syracuse tied the game later in the period when Morris took a pitch and scooted into the end zone from the 6.

Early in the second quarter the raucous crowd saw three touchdowns scored in a dizzying span of 34 seconds. Ken Mandeville plunged across from the 1 to put the Orangemen ahead 14-7, but on the first play after the kickoff Jones broke free for an 82-yard touchdown jaunt. Doing the Redskins one better, Syracuse didn't even need to go on offense to reply, as Morris returned the ensuing kickoff 94 yards for a touchdown.

The kickoff-return touchdown was Syracuse's first since one by Floyd Little in 1965. It was one of Morris's four touchdowns, and it helped him gain 300 all-purpose yards in the game, 170 of which came via the ground on 32 carries, still the most rushing attempts ever by a back in the Dome.

"We had a new quarterback, Dave Warner [who was taking over for the graduated Bill Hurley], it was his first game, and he had a huge act to follow because Hurley was a magnificent quarterback," said Maloney. "Warner had minimal experience and he got the job done, but we went into the game relying on our running game and they couldn't control Joe Morris."

Syracuse extended its lead to 27-14 when an interception by Ike Bogosian at the Miami 22 set up a one-yard TD run by Morris, and then in the final 1:30 the Orangemen drove from their own 27 to the Miami 5, and Anderson kicked a 22-yard field goal for a 30-14 halftime cushion.

Both teams seemed to slow down because of the humid air inside the Dome, and the second half was far less eventful. Jeff Stone's 24-yard field goal was the only score of the third quarter, but the fans began to squirm five minutes into the fourth when the Redskins pulled within 30-24.

Syracuse had stopped Jones on a fourth-and-goal play from the 1 a few minutes earlier, bringing an ear-popping roar from the crowd. But when the Orangemen couldn't drive out and were forced to punt, the Redskins took over at the 50, and this time Hauck took them the distance with an 18-yard touchdown pass to Jay Peterson.

The Orangemen needed to respond, and thanks primarily to Morris—who had brought down the curtain at Archbold with a 203-yard rushing game in the victory over Navy the last time Syracuse played in Syracuse—they did. "Coach said to me 'We're stalling out,' " Morris said. "And me, I took that personally because coach Maloney is like a father to me and I don't want to see him hurt. He stuck his neck out for me. You don't bring 5-foot-7 backs in to play major college football, so I told him I'd get it back."

Morris converted a crucial third-and-5 from the Miami 45 with a seven-yard slam into the line, and after freshman Jamie Covington picked up a first down, Morris took a pitch, bounced off one tackler, sprinted down the right sideline, and dove across the goal line just before being tackled. A two-point conversion pass failed, but with just 4:38 remaining, the Orangemen were safe.

"This game meant a lot to our program," said Morris. "Winning the game was so much more important than the opening of the Dome."

Perhaps on that night, to that group of Syracuse players, that may have been the sentiment, but given what has taken place under that air-supported Teflon-coated roof over the past quarter of a century, the opening of the Dome was the most important development in Syracuse sports history.

During the seventy-plus seasons Syracuse played its football games at Arch-bold, it accrued an impressive record of 265-112-20, including dominant stretches of 61-10-6 between 1915 and 1927 and 47-6-0 between 1958 and 1968. An estimated 6 million people passed through the turnstiles in those seven-plus decades. At the Dome the football team, through the end of the 2004 season, has played in front of nearly 6.5 million people and has a record of 103-44-2, including a school record 16-game home winning streak from 1987 to 1989.

Orange Slice—Joe Morris

A few years ago Joe Morris was asked in an interview who his favorite coach was during his fabulous football career, and the answer was not Bill Parcells, with whom Morris won a Super Bowl following the 1986 NFL season. "Frank Maloney from Syracuse," Morris responded. "I wasn't sure if I was going to play pro ball, but he was the first one to tell me I was going to." Maloney was also the first coach to tell the five-foot-seven Morris that he was going to play major college football.

Morris began his high school career in Southern Pines, North Carolina, before his father, a career military man who served in the Airborne and the Green Berets, was transferred to a base in Ayer, Massachusetts. It was in Ayer, a small town north of Boston, where the late Dave Zuccarelli, Maloney's defensive backs coach, first saw Morris play. As Maloney recalled:

> Dave was responsible for recruiting that area and he came back and told me he really liked this Morris kid, and liked him as a person. So I asked Dave "Who's after him?" and the list wasn't too impressive. I said "You mean Boston College isn't after him?"
>
> But I looked at him on film and he was very impressive, he had that tremendous acceleration and we wound up signing him. If we hadn't, he probably would have gone to the University of New Hampshire.

Morris went on to play four years at Syracuse, the last under Dick MacPherson, and he still holds Orange records for rushing yards in a ca-

More than two decades since he graduated, Joe Morris remains Syracuse's all-time leading rusher with 4,299 yards. He is the only player in school history to have three 1,000-yard rushing seasons.

reer (4,299), season (1,372 in 1979), and game (252 versus Kansas in 1979) as well as attempts in a career (813) and season (261 in 1981, tied with Larry Csonka, 1967). He also leads Syracuse with 22 career 100-yard games and a career average per game of 113.1 yards. With his 278 yards receiving and 1,023 yards on punt returns, Morris is also the school's all-time leader in all-purpose yards, with 5,581.

"He took a chance on me, because no one else in Division I wanted a 5-foot-7 running back," said Morris.

Morris went on to become a second-round draft choice of the New York Giants in 1982, then coached by Ray Perkins. Parcells took over in 1983, and Morris's career blossomed. In 1985 he gained 1,336 and led the NFL with 21 rushing touchdowns, and then in '86 he gained a career-high 1,516 yards—second in the league to Eric Dickerson's 1,821—and added another 313 in the playoffs as the Giants won Super Bowl XXII.

After a third 1,000-yard season in 1988 enabled him to become New York's all-time leading ground gainer, Morris broke his foot in 1989 and missed the entire season, then was waived in 1990 and sat out a year before ending his career with Cleveland in 1991.

Joe Morris

Date of birth: September 15, 1960

Hometown: Fort Bragg, North Carolina

Honors: 1980 ECAC player of the year. . . . Member of SU's All-Century Team.

Achievements: Still ranks number one on SU's all-time rushing list, with 4,299 yards. . . . Still holds record for most yards in a season (1,372) and a game (252). . . . Went on to play eight years in the NFL and won a Super Bowl ring with the Giants.

SU career totals: 4,299 rushing yards, 5,581 all-purpose yards, 27 touchdowns.

10

Triple the Pleasure

March 7, 1981   *Before the Big East Conference basketball*
Carrier Dome   *tournament established a permanent home*
Syracuse, New York   *at Madison Square Garden in 1983, the*
event was held at rotating sites. In 1981
the sparkling new Carrier Dome played
host, and the locals hoisted the hardware
thanks to a triple-overtime conquest of
Villanova.

Leo Rautins was eleven years old when he was told by doctors that not only would he never be able to play sports again but there was also a good chance he might not ever walk again. "That tells you what doctors know," said Rautins, who nine years later was not only walking but also playing Division I basketball for Syracuse University and scoring one of the most memorable baskets in school history.

"That was a wild game," Rautins said in reference to the Orangemen's 83-80 triple-overtime victory over Villanova in the 1981 Big East Tournament championship game at the Carrier Dome. "I've never played in a game like that. Both teams could have put that game away in regulation and in each consecutive overtime. It was one of those games where you went from despair to joy about 15 times. It was just a weird game, and it kept going and going."

Until Rautins ended it by tipping in the rebound of Erich Santifer's missed jumper with two seconds remaining in the third extra period. "That last tap was a super one," said Villanova coach Rollie Massimino, who sealed his own team's fate when he called a timeout just after the

Leo Rautins, a player ahead of his time, was a six-foot-eight ball-handling, smooth-shooting, assist-making guard/forward.

ball fell through the hoop. Problem was, the Wildcats were out of time-outs, so the Orangemen were awarded a technical free throw that Danny Schayes sank to produce the final three-point margin. "That's college basketball."

Rautins grew up in the hockey hotbed of the world, Toronto, but rather than wear blades on his feet, he wore high-top sneakers. Like the rest of the Lithuanian kids in Toronto, Rautins preferred basketball to hockey, and he spent every waking moment bouncing that round ball on the hardwood. "Basketball is our sport," said Rautins. "All the Lithuanian kids, that's what we do, we play hoops. We grew up in a place where nobody was playing basketball except the Lithuanian kids. We'd go to tournaments in the states and play against other Lithuanian teams. We had an open gym all the time when kids normally didn't have one. That brought me into the game, and my brother George played, and I wanted to be better than him."

But while George Rautins was showing off his skills at Niagara University, his little brother was having trouble walking and dealing with nonstop pain in his legs and back.

> The pain was unbearable. My right leg was deteriorating in terms of getting thinner, I wasn't able to put my heel down properly when I walked. I couldn't sit or stand in any position for any length of time without pain shooting through my legs.
>
> It was basically crippling me, and had they not figured out what it was, it could have crippled me. It was an odd thing because people thought I was faking. It took about a year to find out what it was, and I honestly couldn't give you a detailed description of exactly what it was, other than to say that they had never seen anything like it. It was a really unusual condition with spinal fluid being blocked, and fortunately they got to it and corrected it.

It was just before his surgery at a Toronto children's hospital when the neurosurgeon who performed the operation warned Rautins and his parents that there was a chance he could lose the use of his legs, and, even if the procedure was a success, an athletic career was out of the question. "When someone tells you that at our age now, you're walking on pins and needles and you're not going to be doing anything stupid and you're going to be scared to death," said Rautins, who remembered that his parents were definitely scared to death. "But as an 11-year-old you're like 'Yeah whatever.' As soon as you can you're out in the schoolyard running around and playing, you're not worried about it. Ignorance is bliss and that's something that helped me get through that."

The surgery was performed in February 1972, and by that spring

Rautins was pretty much as good as new. "It got to the point where I was moving and I was pain free and feeling good and they didn't have the heart to tell me that I couldn't do things anymore because I seemed to be OK," he said.

So he resumed his basketball career and earned a scholarship to the University of Minnesota, but after one year playing with future NBA star Kevin McHale and leading the Gophers in assists, Rautins quit school because he wasn't enamored with his all-around college experience.

He was going to transfer to Marshall to play for coach Stu Aberdeen, but Aberdeen died of a heart attack just before Rautins enrolled. Syracuse coach Jim Boeheim had recruited Rautins, and when he learned of the six-foot-eight playmaker's dilemma, he called and said a scholarship was waiting if he wanted it. Rautins did, and after sitting out a year because of transfer regulations, Rautins started for the 1980–1981 team, which was playing its second year in the newly formed Big East Conference.

That was not a particularly memorable season, for the Orangemen or for Rautins. Having lost Roosevelt Bouie and Louis Orr to graduation, the team struggled much of the year with a young cast of characters, and Rautins had trouble fitting in. Following a shocking loss at St. Bonaventure that dropped the Orangemen to 10-6 overall, Boeheim summoned Rautins to the front of the bus.

> I remember we lost in Olean and I stunk, and Boeheim said "I have to bench you." I told him "I understand, I'd bench me, too." The only thing I asked is that I'd like a chance to get my job back and try to understand why I'm playing the way I'm playing. I didn't play for a little while, some games I didn't even get in, but he kept his promise and I worked in a lot of other areas and worked hard in practice and right around the Big East tournament he gave me a chance to get my job back and it paid off.

It certainly did. Rautins knew he had gotten his groove back, and he even called his parents in Toronto and told them to come down to Syracuse for the tournament.

> A few games before the Big East tournament we started feeling a little better and playing a little better. Going into the tournament, it was at the

Carrier Dome, and as badly as we played, and even personally it was not a good year for me, walking into the Dome we felt like it was our tournament. There was something weird about it, we had a great feeling about it.

I wanted my folks to come down because, like I said, I had a good feeling. Honestly, your parents take things hard and they knew I was struggling and it was almost like they didn't want to see any more struggling, but I said, "No, come down, you've got to come down for this." I just had a real good feeling."

Syracuse dispatched St. John's in the first round, but Rautins suffered a knee injury when Wayne McCoy of the Redmen barreled into him. "I was there waiting for him and it was one of those old school things where he was looking me right in the eyes and saying `You want to take this one? OK, enjoy it,' " said Rautins, who learned after the season that he had a torn anterior cruciate ligament that would require surgery. "He came right down on top of my knee and it was bad. I finished the game but I was hurting."

He spent that night in the campus infirmary and before the next day's game against Georgetown (a 67-53 win) and then the championship game against Villanova, Syracuse trainer Don Lowe had to spend a couple hours with Rautins to get him physically ready to play.

In the final Syracuse jumped to an early lead, held a 35-33 edge at intermission, then extended its advantage to 51-45 with about 10 minutes left to play. But Massimino's scrappy team clawed back, and a mistake by Rautins helped the Wildcats force the first overtime. Eddie Moss made two free throws with 1:04 remaining to give Syracuse a three-point lead, but Rautins was whistled for early entry into the lane, wiping out the second free throw. Alex Bradley then hit a foul-line jumper with 20 ticks left in regulation.

In the first overtime Villanova seemed destined to win. It opened a 70-64 lead, but Moss hit from the lane, and after Villanova's John Pinone missed the front end of a one-and-one, Moss fed Schayes for a layup to make it 70-68, and the crowd of 15,213 roared its glee. After a time-out, Santifer—in the starting lineup for the tournament because Marty Headd had suffered a broken wrist in practice earlier in the week—stole the ball from Tom Sienkiewicz. Santifer drove in and missed a layup, but

Moss was there for the tying tip-in, and when neither team scored again it was on to the second overtime.

This time it was Syracuse taking charge at 78-74 with 1:06 to go, but Sienkiewicz hit a jumper, and after a Syracuse turnover Bradley knocked down an eighteen-footer to tie it with 18 seconds remaining. Santifer had a chance to win it at the horn but missed, and Moss's tip-in rolled around the rim and fell off.

The third overtime was a stall fest. Schayes won the tip, and the Orangemen held the ball for more than three minutes before Schayes was fouled. He made both shots, only to see Stewart Granger tie it at 80. Syracuse then controlled the ball the rest of the way, and after a time-out with 8 seconds remaining, Boeheim called for Rautins to take the final shot. He did, but not the way it was drawn up.

> I was taking it out on the side in front of our bench. I'd had a pretty good tournament [he was named MVP], so the play was for me to get it in to Santifer somewhere around the top of the key and halfcourt, and then I was going to get the ball back and take the shot. This is the benefit of knowing your teammates, I guess, because when Erich got the ball, I knew it wasn't coming back.
>
> He's a big competitor, he got the ball and just the way the defense played him I knew he was going to try to make a play. Aaron Howard was covering me on the inbounds and he made the mistake that a lot of players make—he forgot about the inbounds passer. He turned to see where the ball went, and kind of moved to the ball. As soon as Erich got the ball he put it on the floor and started going toward the foul line. I knew what he was going to do so I just went to the basket. Sure enough he shot it and the ball bounced literally right into my hands.

Although the Dome was barely half-filled, the noise was deafening, and up in the stands were Rautins' parents, jumping up and down. "I had hit some game winners before, but this was the Big East tournament," Rautins said. "Coming from where we came from as a team, and where I had come from individually, putting it all together was pretty cool."

The elation of this victory didn't even last twenty-four hours because the next day Syracuse was spurned by the NCAA Tournament Selection Committee.

The Big East Tournament winner was not granted an automatic berth into what was then the forty-eight-team NCAA Tournament until 1981–1982, and with a 15-11 record the Orangemen lost out to Big East rivals Villanova, Boston College, and Georgetown. Syracuse accepted a bid to the NIT and reeled off three victories before losing to Tulsa 86-84 in overtime in the championship game at Madison Square Garden.

As for Rautins, a player truly ahead of his time, he recorded the first triple-double in Big East history in 1983 and upon graduation was a first-round pick of the Philadelphia 76ers. His NBA career never took off, though, and after spending several years in Europe, he came back to the United States, settled down in Syracuse, and now works as a broadcaster on Toronto Raptors games and does occasional work for ESPN.

Orange Slice—Danny Schayes

If you had lined them up side by side during the three years they played together at Syracuse, it would have been a no-brainer. With his long, lithe seven-foot frame and his ability to block shots at one end of the floor and make them at the other, you would have taken one look and predicted that Roosevelt Bouie would go on to enjoy a long and prosperous career in the NBA. With his thick six-foot-eleven body that he preferred to station away from the basket from where he could shoot jumpers and pass, you would have concluded that the only way Danny Schayes was going to make money playing basketball was over in Europe.

So what happened? Bouie graduated from Syracuse in 1980, was a second-round pick of the Dallas Mavericks, spurned their offer, and took his talents overseas, where he forged a dynamic sixteen-year career far away from the bright lights of the NBA. Schayes, who didn't start at Syracuse until his senior year after Bouie had departed, became a first-round draft pick of the Utah Jazz and went on to play an incredible eighteen years in the NBA, averaging 7.7 points and 5.0 rebounds in 1,138 games for Utah, Denver, Milwaukee, the Lakers, Phoenix, Miami, and Orlando.

Schayes grew up in Jamesville and dreamed of playing at Syracuse, but when his storied high school career was over, his father, Dolph—who had been an NBA star with the old Syracuse Nationals—suggested

Danny Schayes was a high school standout at Jamesville-Dewitt who decided to stay in town and attend Syracuse. He didn't become a starter until his senior season, but he played so well that year that it set the stage for an eighteen-year NBA career.

he enroll elsewhere. Dolph thought playing at home would be too stressful for his son, as Orange fans would expect too much given his last name.

That is, of course, if he ever made it onto the court. Bouie had enjoyed a superb freshman season, and Dolph warned Danny that Bouie was going to be Syracuse's center for the next three years, thus curtailing Danny's playing time. However, against the advice of his father and Orange assistant Rick Pitino, Schayes chose Syracuse. It proved to be an inspired decision.

As predicted, Schayes didn't start his first three years, though he was a key reserve on three straight NCAA Tournament teams. More important, his game improved as he battled daily with Bouie in practice, and it was that work that ultimately prepared Schayes for the rigors of the NBA. "For Danny, practice was as competitive as the games," Louis Orr told Mike Waters in his recent book *Legends of Syracuse Basketball*. "That was the key to his success. His road wasn't easy, but in the long run it probably made him better to play against Roosevelt every day. I know that helped make Danny a better player."

When Schayes finally became the starter in 1980–1981, he produced a terrific season, averaging 14.6 points and 8.3 rebounds per game. NBA scouts took notice, particularly when Schayes earned MVP honors at a postseason seniors-only tournament in Hawaii.

The 1981 draft was not a deep one for centers, and Schayes wound up going in the first round (number thirteen overall), with only Oregon State University center Steve Johnson picked ahead of him.

Danny Schayes

Date of birth: May 10, 1959

Hometown: Syracuse, New York

Honors: All-American in 1981. . . . 1981 Post-Graduate Scholarship winner. . . . First-team All–Big East in 1981.

Achievements: Led SU in scoring, rebounds, and blocked shots in 1980–1981. . . . Made 80.6 percent of his career free throws. . . . Had 23-rebound game against Georgetown in 1981, tied for SU's best in a Big East game. . . . Enjoyed an eighteen-year career in the NBA.

SU career totals: 964 points, 635 rebounds, 134 blocked shots.

11

The Day the Jays
Turned Blue

May 28, 1983   *Syracuse's first modern-day lacrosse na-*
Rutgers Stadium   *tional championship in 1983 was its most*
New Brunswick, New Jersey   *improbable as the Orangemen rallied from*
                      a seven-goal third-quarter deficit to defeat
                      Johns Hopkins, officially stamping Roy
                      Simmons Jr.'s program as a national
                      power.

It was halftime of the 1983 NCAA Division I lacrosse championship game, and coach Henry Ciccarone led his front-running Johns Hopkins University team into the well-deserved coolness of the air-conditioned locker room.

On the other side of the field, Syracuse coach Roy Simmons Jr., frustrated by his team's 8-4 deficit and the way the Orangemen had played in the first thirty minutes, ordered his players to sit right there on the sideline and continue to bake in the ninety-degree heat that was suffocating Rutgers Stadium. "Here's the crowd, here's the scoreboard," Simmons said. "There's no sanctuary."

Up in the press box, a smile creased the eighty-two-year-old face of Roy Simmons Sr., a smile almost as effervescent as the one he wore later that day when his son's team—after falling behind by seven goals in the third quarter—stormed back in the fourth quarter to pull off a remarkable 17-16 victory, giving Syracuse its first lacrosse championship since 1925 when Roy Sr. was an All-American defenseman.

Roy Simmons Jr. and Syracuse chancellor Melvin Eggers pose in 1983 with the first of the six national championship trophies Simmons won during his tenure on the Orange sideline.

After watching the Orangemen sputter against the formidable but certainly not invincible Blue Jays, Roy Sr. remarked at halftime that he would have done the same thing. Would have let 'em bake in the heat. Of course, old Roy would have mixed in some scintillating play-by-play laced with colorful language, and he might have slapped a few helmets and thrown a few sticks for good measure.

That wasn't his son's style. Roy Jr. was never into machismo. He wasn't much of a screamer and yeller. He was a teacher, a strategist, analytical and caring. A sentimental man who found just as much thrill sculpting fine pieces of art as he did winning lacrosse championships, Roy Jr. didn't buy into the "bend 'em till they break" style of coaching that worked so effectively for his father over the four decades Roy Sr. served as Syracuse's legendary head lacrosse coach.

But on that day, in that stadium, under that blazing sun, with that

1983 team, which has always held a special place in Roy Jr.'s heart, he knew a chalk talk wasn't going to roust the Orangemen from their slumber. And therein lies the beauty and the brilliance of the man his players were comfortable enough to call him by his nickname, "Slugger." He always knew how to reach his team, always knew which buttons to push.

That 1983 team was as close-knit a group as he ever coached. He knew it would respond to this old-school tactic because he knew this ensemble was embarrassed by what had happened in those first thirty minutes and would summon all its pride and spirit in an effort to make amends in the second half.

"At halftime I think coach Simmons did a great job of keeping everyone's head in the game, keeping us focused, and I think everybody came out in the second half saying 'Hey, if we keep playing hard, keep fighting like we've been fighting all season, we can claw our way back into this,' " recalled Brad Kotz, then a sophomore midfielder who fought like no other, scoring five goals in the final two quarters to help fuel the greatest rally in championship game history. "What I remember about that team was the tightness and the camaraderie that we had for one another. We may not have been the greatest lacrosse players in the country that year, but as a team we kind of transcended our individual qualities and basically became a much better group than the individuals would have been on their own."

When Simmons took over the Syracuse program from his father in 1971, it was not the glamorous job it became. There were no scholarships. There was no funding from the Athletic Department. Simmons sometimes had to comb the campus looking for players to fill out the roster. To raise money for road trips his players sold raffle tickets door to door. One time Syracuse had to borrow a spare goalie stick from the team it was playing, Cornell.

The program endured three straight losing seasons in the mid-1970s, something that had never happened during Roy Sr.'s forty-year tenure. During the worst season in school history, the 2-9 campaign of 1974, Cornell beat the Orangemen 27-4.

But Roy Jr. persevered. He remained patient. He overcame all the obstacles and was able to convince many of the talented kids who grew up playing at area high schools such as Camillus powerhouse West Genesee that Syracuse was the place to be.

One of those players was Kotz, who was coming off a New York State Championship in 1981 at West Genesee and could have chosen a number of schools to attend, including—thanks to his excellent grades—a couple in the Ivy League. He chose Syracuse. "A lot of it had to do with coach Simmons," said Kotz, who today lives in Maryland and owns his own real estate development company. "He became a good friend of mine my senior year in high school and he was a guy I really wanted to play for. His bond with the players was so special in so many ways and I wanted to be part of that."

The '83 team was comprised of Kotz and nine other West Genesee grads plus college transfers from four schools, one of whom was Tim Nelson, a Long Island native who migrated back to the North after a year at North Carolina State. "He's not a loudmouth coach like a lot of coaches who came to see me," said Nelson, now the head lacrosse coach at Division III Utica College. "He spoke honestly to me, like a real person."

The NCAA Lacrosse Tournament came into existence in 1971, and Syracuse did not earn an invitation until 1979. After making it three years in a row, reaching the Final Four in 1980, it had missed the party in 1982, Kotz's freshman year, so 1983 was targeted as a year for redemption. But no one could have imagined a national championship, certainly not when Hopkins jumped out to a 12-5 lead in the third quarter.

"That team had a chemistry like no other team I played on," said Kotz of the '83 club that also included players such as Randy Lundblad, Art Lux, Jeff McCormick, Dave Desko, Tom Korrie, and goalie Travis Solomon. "We had some role players, we had great leadership, we had an underdog mentality because the prior year we didn't make it into the playoffs, and personally that was something that was eating at me all season. But that being said, I don't think the expectation was there for us, so we were out there to prove something that entire year."

The Orangemen won their first seven games, lost at Army, then won four in a row to cruise into the NCAAs with an 11-1 record. No one knew it at the time, but when Syracuse eliminated Penn, 11-8, to reach the semifinals, it started an unprecedented streak of twenty-two consecutive appearances in the Final Four, a feat that was finally stopped when the Orange lost in the first round of the 2005 NCAA Tournament.

At that time the semifinals were played at home sites, and the Orangemen, playing host in the Carrier Dome, whipped Maryland, 12-5, to earn a trip to Rutgers for a showdown with Johns Hopkins. The Blue Jays would be playing in their seventh straight championship game, and Kotz confirms now what he knew then: "They were the team to beat, no question."

Early on, it did not look as if Syracuse was capable of doing it. The number one–ranked Blue Jays scored the first three goals, and by midway through the second quarter it was 7-2 before goals by Lundblad and Lux helped pull Syracuse within 8-4 at the break.

"The first half, I can remember leading three or four, maybe five fast breaks and we weren't converting," said Kotz, who like Simmons is a member of the National Lacrosse Hall of Fame. "We were getting broken situations and we weren't finishing them. That was frustrating because as a transitional midfielder I kind of prided myself on that style of game. At halftime I was kind of pent up that we had opportunities we didn't capitalize on."

After stewing in the searing heat, the Orangemen came stumbling out to start the third quarter as Johns Hopkins answered a quick Lundblad goal with four in a row to bump its cushion to the seemingly insurmountable 12-5.

And then defenseman Darrin Lawlor, of all people, beat Johns Hopkins goalie Brian Holman for an unassisted goal, and the tide changed in an instant. Before the third quarter was finished Syracuse had three more goals, including one by Kotz, to cut its deficit to 13-9. "I felt like we were controlling the tempo of the game and in the third quarter we started to control the ball a lot more," said Kotz. That's because Hopkins, comfortably ahead and feeling confident, seemed to lose interest.

"The worst thing that could have happened to Hopkins was getting that big lead," said Simmons Jr. "They had lost their intensity. They couldn't measure the intensity of our team. They thought the fire was out." Added Nelson: "When they got up by all those goals they just started throwing the ball out of bounds. You could see it in their eyes. They didn't think this game was such a big deal. It just didn't seem like they cared anymore."

That became apparent in the fourth quarter. The Blue Jays were listless, and Syracuse ripped off six straight goals—three by Kotz and one each by Nelson, Desko, and Korrie—in the first 5:32 to surge ahead by

15-13. "One thing we did all season, when we started a rally, the team built off of that and we'd typically respond with a few more goals," said Kotz. "That was a characteristic of our team. Once we got into a groove, we could carry that groove for half a period or a period and I think we got there in the third and fourth. There was definitely some added focus in the second half."

Johns Hopkins managed to score twice on Solomon—who had shaken off a sloppy first half to play an inspired second half—to tie the score, but Kotz scored his fifth of the day unassisted with 2:36 to go, then Nelson recorded his sixth assist and eighth point of the day, feeding Lundblad on the crease for the goal that proved to be the winner with 1:09 remaining.

Del Dressel threw a scare into the Orangemen when he scored 19 seconds later, but the Orange controlled the ensuing face-off and were able to burn the rest of the clock. "I just remember the pure desire that we all shared on that field, and that was mostly evident in the second half," said Kotz, who received the ultimate honor in 2001 when he was enshrined in the National Lacrosse Hall of Fame.

When the Orangemen were finally allowed to go indoors and escape the heat, Roy Sr. was waiting for them. "To come back like that was magnificent," said the patriarch of Syracuse lacrosse. "I have never seen a comeback like that against such a great team."

And that's when his son did something he had dreamed of doing. He took the national championship plaque, held it aloft as his players cheered gleefully, and handed it to his father. "The only time I ever saw him cry," Roy Jr. said. "And he said 'Thank God that He let me live long enough to see you be a champion.' "

It was on that day that the Syracuse lacrosse dynasty—a lacrosse record nine national championships and counting—was born. Syracuse returned to the Final Four each of the next four years, but it lost the next two championship games at Johns Hopkins in 1984 and '85, and then lost twice in the semifinals to Virginia (1986) and Cornell (1987). Kotz and Nelson each became three-time first-team All-Americans, Nelson still sits atop the all-time Orange list with 187 assists, and Kotz scored 129 goals and 205 points. In conjunction with the 1997 Final Four, the NCAA Lacrosse Committee chose a twenty-fifth-anniversary team, and both Kotz and Nelson, as well as Gary Gait and Paul Gait, were selected.

Orange Slice—Tim Nelson

It should come as no surprise to anyone who ever played with Tim Nelson that he is Syracuse's record holder for assists—career, single season, and single game. "Tim was a great all-around athlete with a great sense of confidence, and he understands the team side of sports," said his teammate for three years at Syracuse, Brad Kotz. "So many guys come through and are great individual performers, but he engaged everybody else in what he did. He would have succeeded in any sport. He understood the mentality of team sports. It was a pleasure to play with him."

Not surprisingly, in the only championship game the Orangemen won during Nelson's three years on the Hill, he assisted on six goals, five coming in the second half when the Orangemen put on their momentous rally to defeat Johns Hopkins. Fittingly, his final assist, on a goal by Randy Lundblad, was the goal that ultimately clinched the 17-16 victory.

By the time Nelson graduated from Syracuse with a bachelor's degree in psychology and a master's degree in higher education administration, he was one of the Orange's most decorated players. He was a three-time All-American and a three-time winner of the Turnbull Award, which is given to the top attackman in the nation by the United States Intercollegiate Lacrosse Association.

Nelson still ranks number one in career assists with 187, he is the only player in Syracuse history to record 9 assists in one game (he did it on three occasions), and he owns the three best single-season assist marks (67 in 1984, 64 in 1985, and 56 in 1983). Among the Gait and Powell brothers, the closest anyone comes to Nelson's records are Ryan Powell, who had 51 assists in 2000 and 150 assists for his career, and Casey Powell, who had 8 assists in a game against Loyola in 1997.

Today, Nelson shares his team-oriented philosophies with the Utica College men's lacrosse program, continuing a coaching career that spans twenty years since his graduation. He began as an assistant under Roy Simmons at Syracuse from 1985 to 1987 and was an assistant at the University of North Carolina at Chapel Hill for three years before serving a ten-year stint as head coach at Dartmouth College. After leaving the Big Green he worked as an assistant at Nazareth under his younger

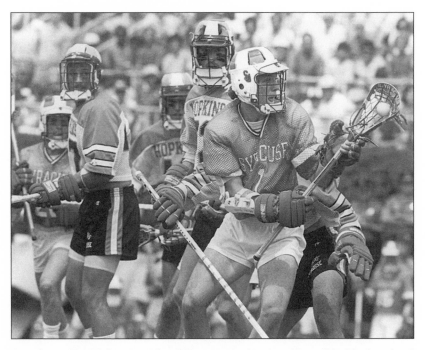

Attackman Tim Nelson was the ultimate assist king, and he still holds the school records for helpers in a game, season, and career.

brother, Scott, before taking over the Utica program in 2000. "Our vision is to do what Syracuse did for lacrosse," Nelson said of the Division III Utica program. "We want to build the program, yes, but we want to build lacrosse in the area. Since lacrosse started at UC, I've seen a growth in the local programs. We do a lot to promote lacrosse in the whole area."

Tim Nelson

Date of birth: May 25, 1963

Hometown: Yorktown, New York

Honors: Three-time winner (1983–1985) of the Turnbull Award given to nation's top attackman. . . . Three-time first-team All-America (1983–1985). . . . Selected to the NCAA's twenty-fifth-anniversary team that was chosen in 1997.

Achievements: Is still SU's all-time assists leader for career (187), season (67), and game (9). . . . His 103 points in 1984 remains the SU single-season record. . . . Had three 9-assist games, and has the three highest single-season assist totals in SU history (67, 64, 56).

SU career totals: 84 goals, 187 assists, 271 points.

12

A Gem of a Shot
by the Pearl

January 21, 1984   *Midway through his freshman season,*
Carrier Dome   *Pearl Washington etched himself indelibly*
Syracuse, New York   *into Syracuse lore when he launched a shot*
from half-court that swished through the
net as the buzzer sounded, giving the Or-
ange an incredible victory over Boston
College.

Nearly two decades since his Nikes last squeaked against the Carrier Dome hardwood, Dwayne "Pearl" Washington continues to
be asked about "the shot heard 'round the college basketball world."
And each time someone inquires about his buzzer-beating, game-
winning, half-court heave, a Dome-sized smile creases Pearl's face. "I
never tire of talking about it," said the man who was the most publi-
cized recruit in Syracuse University history. "That shot made me a permanent part of Syracuse basketball. I had so many great moments
during my playing days there, but that one's hard to top." Indeed it is.

For as long as shots are flung beneath SU's Teflon-coated, air-
supported big top, people will talk about Pearl's signature moment fifteen games into his freshman season. And they'll reminisce about the
fandemonium that followed. Minutes after Washington's shot defeated
Boston College, 75-73, SU senior co-captain Sean Kerins proclaimed:
"The Pearl has arrived."

Actually, his legend preceded him to the Syracuse campus. Re-

Pearl Washington brought a never-before-seen flair to the Carrier Dome, and Jim Boeheim's most-prized recruit (until Carmelo Anthony came along in 2002) thrilled the masses with his entertaining brand of basketball.

cruited by more than two hundred college basketball programs, the All-American point guard from Brooklyn's Boys and Girls High School announced his decision to attend the 'Cuse during a nationally televised game in March 1983.

Pearl's decision resulted in three thousand additional basketball season-ticket sales at SU and guaranteed a record six thirty thousand–plus crowds for his freshman campaign on the Hill. "Dwayne has gotten everyone excited," SU coach Jim Boeheim said at the time. "If I were a fan, I'd pay to see him, too."

A chunky six-foot-two guard, Washington was coveted because of his Harlem Globetrotter–like dribbling skills and his sleight-of-hand passes. While watching the Pearl average thirty-five points, ten rebounds, eight assists, and four steals per game as a high school senior, Boeheim observed, "Dwayne's so good right now, he could penetrate against an NBA guard." Former NBA champion player and coach Larry Costello called Washington "a miniature Oscar Robertson. He can do what he wants to on the basketball court. You just can't guard him one-on-one. And he sees the entire court so well."

While comparisons to Basketball Hall of Famers like the "Big O" were flattering, Washington liked it best when people mentioned him in the same breath as his idol, Earl "the Pearl" Monroe. Friends in his Brooklyn neighborhood pinned the nickname of the former New York Knick great on Washington after watching him display his fancy dribbling skills on the glass-strewn, bent-rim asphalt playground courts of the Big Apple. "I had dinner with [Monroe] when I was in high school," Washington recalled. "He told me how to become a great scorer. He said, 'Dwayne, it's simple. Just score 10 points each quarter.' "

For every high school phenom who makes the transition to college superstardom, there are scores of others who fade into oblivion, never to be heard from again. But Washington, who had been a man among boys in the stuffy gymnasiums of New York City, was confident he'd be able to bridge the talent gap between scholastic hoops and the Big East Conference. "People ask me if I'm feeling pressure because everybody is expecting so much from me this year and I tell them no," Washington said on the eve of his college debut. "After all the recruiting and media coverage I've had since I was an eighth-grader, I know I can handle this." Still, he didn't—as Kerins pointed out—"arrive" as a bona fide Syracuse sports legend until he hit that shot against Boston College.

With a nine-point lead with fifteen minutes remaining, it didn't appear as if the Orangemen were going to need any last-second heroics to down their Big East rival. The Eagles stormed back to take the lead briefly, but Kerins converted two corner jumpers and passed to Rafael Addison for a dunk to put SU up 73-69 with fifty-three seconds remaining.

Moments later, BC forward Jay Murphy tipped in a missed shot to cut the deficit to two. With twenty-six seconds to go Kerins missed the front end of a one-and-one, and Boston College grabbed the rebound. The Eagles brought the ball upcourt and tied the game on Martin Clark's jumper with four seconds left. To make matters worse, Clark was fouled on the play, giving BC an excellent chance to take the lead and probably win the game. But his free-throw attempt bounced off the front of the rim and into the hands of Kerins. "At that point," Boeheim said. "I figured we were going into overtime." His sentiments were shared by the 30,293 spectators and all the players. All the players, that is, except for Washington.

Kerins passed the ball to Pearl who dribbled past Clark and let fly with the shot just as he passed the half-court line. The forty-five-footer swished through the basket just as the horn sounded. With his fist raised in celebration, the beaming Washington continued running off the court and through the tunnel leading to the locker room, wisely avoiding the stampede of adoring fans.

The instant the shot dropped through the basket, an ecstatic Boeheim leaped about four feet into the air and did a victory jig on his way to the locker room. "I never jumped that high when I was playing," he said moments later. "I could have slam-dunked the ball tonight."

Long before it became fashionable to storm the court, thousands of delirious fans jumped over the tables along press row and onto the hardwood. Some, no doubt taking a cue from their football brethren, attempted unsuccessfully to rip down the basket that had graciously accepted Washington's historic shot.

It marked the first time the Orangemen had won a buzzer beater since Leo Rautins had tipped in a shot with three seconds remaining in triple overtime in the 1981 Big East Conference final against Villanova. "When I got the ball there wasn't time to pass so I shot instead," said Washington, who finished the night with 20 points and 7 assists. "I knew it was straight-on when I let it go, but I didn't know if it was going to be short or long. When it went in, I almost fainted."

Interestingly, the weakest part of Pearl's game had been his outside shooting. But on this night, he showed he could shoot from the outside. Way outside. "If anyone can make a shot like that, it's Dwayne," Boeheim said. Added junior SU center Andre Hawkins: "That's the kind of thing people expect from Pearl. He's a winner. He finds a way to win."

The USA cable network, which was televising the game, almost missed the climactic moment. When Washington was furiously dribbling up the floor for the last shot, a producer in the control truck outside the Dome tried to anticipate which camera angle to use. He thought for a moment that Pearl might opt to pass upcourt instead of shoot. According to one production assistant, "He almost switched to another player up court. Could you imagine if we had missed a shot like Washington's? Heads would have rolled."

Though he didn't lead the Orangemen to a Final Four, Pearl made an indelible impression that went well beyond his famous game-winning shot. He averaged 15.7 points and 6.7 assists per game while guiding SU to seventy-one victories and three NCAA Tournament appearances while putting the Orange program on the national college basketball map. "He was," said Boeheim, "the reason there was a guy in line waiting to buy that 31,000th seat." He was perhaps the most entertaining player in the school's basketball history and the reason the hottest-selling T-shirt on campus once bore Washington's picture and the words: ". . . On the eighth day God created the Pearl."

He left for the NBA after his junior season and had a nondescript professional career. After battling a serious illness, he returned to campus and completed his studies to earn his degree. He is one of just five SU players—Vic Hanson, Dave Bing, Sherman Douglas, and Wilmeth Sidat-Singh—to have his jersey retired.

Orange Slice—Rafael Addison

The only regret Rafael Addison has about his Syracuse basketball career is the way it ended. He had hoped to finish with a flourish, but a late-season ankle injury against Seton Hall during his senior season short-circuited his dreams of leading the Orangemen to the Final Four. "I still wonder how far we might have gone that year if I hadn't wrecked my ankle," said Addison, who lives back in his native Jersey City, New Jersey, where he teaches elementary school and coaches varsity basketball at his alma mater, Snyder High School. "We were loaded that year. I think we could have gone far."

SU was 18-2 at the time of his injury during that 1985–1986 season and wound up being upset by the David Robinson–led U.S. Naval Academy in the second round of the NCAA Tournament—at the Carrier Dome, no less. Addison, who had averaged 18.4 points per game during his junior year, saw his average slip to 15 per game after the injury.

Still, despite the sour ending, Addison put together one of the finest careers in SU hoops history. A natural-born scorer, the lithe six-foot-seven Addison finished his career with 1,876 points, just 7 shy of Dave Bing's all-time school record. His total still ranks ninth after Hakim Warrick became the most recent player to surpass him, in 2005. "He would have scored a lot more," said coach Jim Boeheim, "had he played in the era of the 3-point shot because he was such an excellent outside shooter."

During Addison's four seasons, the Orangemen compiled a 92-34 record and went to four consecutive NCAA Tournaments, but they never made it past the second round. That ankle injury in his senior season, Boeheim says, was one of the keys to that Syracuse flameout because without Addison at full strength, the Orange simply weren't as potent. "I think it hurt us tremendously," said Boeheim.

Addison never quite found his niche in the NBA. He was a second-round choice of the Phoenix Suns in 1986 and averaged just 5.8 points per game as a rookie. He was cut the following year and went to Europe to continue his professional career. After four seasons abroad he returned to the United States and spent the next five years playing for New Jersey, Detroit, and Charlotte, but he was never a full-time starter and his career average in 379 games wound up being 5.8.

Rafael Addison

Date of birth: July 22, 1964

Hometown: Jersey City, New Jersey

Honors: Honorable mention All-America in 1984, '85, and '86. . . . All–Big East first team in 1985 and second team in '84 and '86. . . . Member of SU All-Century Team. . . . Earned Vic Hanson Medal of Excellence, one of SU's most distinguished awards.

Achievements: Ranked second on SU's all-time scoring list when he graduated in 1986 and still stands ninth. . . . Holds SU single-game record for steals by a freshman, with 7 against Cornell. . . . Scored 5,545 points in NBA career.

SU career totals: 1,876 points, 649 rebounds, 320 assists, 148 steals, and 65 blocked shots.

13

An Upset for the Ages

September 29, 1984 *They have been playing games on the Hill*
Carrier Dome *for more than a century, and there have*
Syracuse, New York *been countless memorable triumphs by*
squads of Orangemen, but only one can
hold the dual titles of most improbable and
most remarkable—the 1984 football vic-
tory over number one–ranked Nebraska.

He could have gone anywhere to play college football. That's how highly regarded Tim Green was back in the fall of 1981. But the erudite young man with the superb athletic skills ultimately decided not to travel far at all—just a few miles south on Interstate 81 from his Liverpool home to Syracuse University.

Green chose the Orangemen over national football juggernaut Penn State because he wanted to be the catalyst in a gridiron resurrection at SU. Coach Dick MacPherson had sold Green on the idea of becoming the cornerstone recruit in the revival, the coveted, magnetic Pied Piper whose very presence would lure other high school standouts to follow in his cleat steps and help make Syracuse an eastern college football power once more. "I was intrigued with the idea of being on the ground floor of something really special," recalled Green, who would become an All-American defensive end and a Rhodes Scholar candidate. "It was an enormous challenge because the program certainly was down at the time. But I saw it as an opportunity to make some history. My teammates and I had a chance to write a memorable chapter."

And so Green signed on the dotted line in February 1982 and that fall

All-American defensive lineman Tim Green exalts in victory in the Syracuse locker room following the triumph over Nebraska. On the wall behind him is the notation "19-0" that had been written by a player the previous week, a reminder of how terrible it felt to lose to Rutgers.

began work on the rough draft of a chapter that remains special all these years later—a chapter that would include the most improbable victory in Syracuse sports history.

A change in SU's football fortunes would not occur immediately. During Green's freshman season it seemed like more of the same for the program as the Orangemen struggled to just 2 wins in 11 games. The next year, with Green and the rest of the defense emerging as a force to be reckoned with, their record improved to 6-5, SU's first winning season since 1979.

That fueled great expectations for the autumn of '84—expectations that were heightened by season-opening victories over Maryland and Northwestern. "We were riding a wave," said Green, a true Renaissance man who is an author, lawyer, and network football analyst. "Then, against Rutgers in the third game, the wave came crashing down against the shore."

The Orangemen entered that game against the visiting Scarlet

Knights as ten-point favorites. But the oddsmakers apparently forgot to tell the Rutgers' players they were supposed to be pushovers that Saturday night in the Carrier Dome. Perhaps the Orangemen were looking ahead to their matchup the following week against top-ranked Nebraska because they clearly lacked focus against Rutgers. They wound up committing eight turnovers, and the Scarlet Knights took advantage of SU's sloppiness to score a 19-0 upset. The putrid performance prompted lusty boos from the Orange unfaithful.

Before leaving the Dome that night, one of the SU players took a marker and wrote "19-0" on the wall above his locker. He easily could have written "63-7" next to it as a painful, motivating reminder of how badly the Cornhuskers had clobbered the Orangemen in Lincoln, Nebraska, the year before.

There was a feeling the Cornhuskers might even exceed that margin of victory in the 1984 meeting between the teams. Las Vegas had installed them as twenty-four-point favorites, and *Sports Illustrated* splashed them on the cover the week of the SU game, calling them "The Big Red Machine."

Although his team had won twenty-four consecutive regular-season games, Nebraska coach Tom Osborne said he was concerned about the matchup with the Orangemen, especially the Green-led defense. "We beat them badly," Osborne told reporters days before the '84 game. "But as I looked at the films I realized it was one of those situations where the score wasn't indicative of the game. We had more trouble blocking Syracuse than anybody we played all year. What I'm trying to do is convince you that this isn't going to be a pushover." Osborne added: "I'd rather be playing a team coming off a win than a loss. I think it will probably bring out the best in Syracuse."

No one seemed to be heeding Osborne's warnings. Nor did anyone seem to be buying the optimism MacPherson was selling in Syracuse. While talking to reporters, he didn't sound at all like a man being led to the gallows. "The matchups are there," MacPherson said. "Their good offense against our good defense. Our offense, which has sputtered, against their pretty good defense. Special teams against special teams. Now, we'll play the game and see what happens."

What happened was the most remarkable upset in the hundred-year-plus history of Syracuse football. An upset that would turn the sports world on its ear. Playing with a ferocity and a precision sorely lacking the week before, the Orangemen totally dominated the number-one 'Huskers en route to a 17-9 victory in front of 47,280 shocked spectators. Many of the same fans who had booed SU off the field following the Rutgers debacle were so appreciative this time around that they demanded a curtain call.

Up in the press box, Ben Schwartzwalder, who had coached SU's '59ers to a national title twenty-five years earlier, leaped to his feet in glee. "I still can't believe it," he said, chomping on an unlit cigar. "This and the Cotton Bowl win over Texas in 1959. . . . That's the only other win I can remember that compares to this one."

Interestingly, the Orangemen didn't rely on any trick plays, funny bounces, or ninety-nine-yard kickoff or interception returns to pull off the upset. They merely lined up and beat the stuffing out of their supposedly stronger opponent. "They won it up front, both offensively and defensively," Osborne admitted. "We got banged around pretty good. Football is a physical game and they were flat out more physical than we were. This victory was not a fluke."

The Cornhuskers had come to Syracuse averaging 531 yards per game. But they were unable to move the ball with any consistency that day in the Dome, finishing with just 214 yards. SU forced them to punt seven times, caused two fumbles, intercepted a pass, and stopped Nebraska cold on a fourth-and-1. Some attributed the Cornhuskers' offensive problems to the absence of star running back Jeff Smith, who missed the game with a sprained ankle. But Osborne, to his credit, refused to make excuses. "I honestly can't say it would have been any different if Jeff Smith played," he said.

Despite SU's dominance, the Cornhuskers led 7-3 at the half, and there was a feeling, even among staunch Orange supporters like Schwartzwalder, that it was only a matter of time before Nebraska went on a scoring binge. "I thought the floodgates would eventually open," ol' Ben said. "But I guess I underestimated how badly our boys wanted it."

MacPherson knew his team was focused even before it boarded the bus for the short trip from its hotel over to the Dome. He watched with pride as running back Jamie Covington, one of the Orange captains, addressed the team. "I don't want to see any Walkmans on the bus," Covington told his teammates. "Take those things off and think of nothing but Nebraska. That's where your total focus should be."

Although the Syracuse offense wasn't as impressive as the Orange defense, it managed to do what was needed to secure the win. Covington bulled his way for 100 rushing yards, but the true hero of the day was beleaguered quarterback Todd Norley. The week before, Norley had been jeered off the field after fumbling three times and throwing two interceptions against Rutgers. He was despondent after that game, but he didn't stay down for long. His roommate, Green, wouldn't allow him to remain bummed out, not with mighty Nebraska on the horizon. "Tim's just the most optimistic person in the world," Norley said. "He joked around and told me that the offense had better do its job against Nebraska because the defense was going to do its job. By Tuesday, I was feeling pretty good about things again."

Roughly five minutes into the third quarter, Norley made one of the most dramatic passes in SU sports history—a play that ultimately would cut the Cornhuskers down to size. Although Nebraska defensive end Scott Strassburger was boring in on him like a raging bull, Norley stood his ground and lofted a pass 40 yards downfield toward the Cornhuskers' end zone. Wide receiver Mike Siano went up over two defenders, caught the ball at the 1, and fell into the end zone for what would prove to be the winning score. "I'm sorry I didn't get a chance to see it," Norley joked afterward. "I was lying flat on my back as a result of the hit. But I could hear the crowd. I knew something good had happened."

Norley wrenched his knee on the play and had to be helped off the field. Few in the crowd thought the quarterback would return, but he did. Norley wound up completing 9 of 18 passes for 108 yards. Though the stats were hardly gaudy, they were good enough.

The Orangemen iced the win late in the fourth quarter when running back Harold Gayden sprinted in from the 1—his path to the end zone cleared by a crunching block by pulling guard Steve Villanti.

After the final gun sounded, fans stormed the field to join in the celebration. In the jubilant Syracuse locker room Norley hammed it up by donning a pair of sunglasses. Green, who recorded two sacks against the 'Huskers, hugged his giddy roommate and called him "Hollywood." "This," Green bellowed above the din, "is why I came to Syracuse. I wanted to be able to experience moments like this one."

Though the Orangemen never won more than seven games during Green's four years there, he clearly was the catalyst for positive change in Syracuse football. MacPherson began landing other blue-chip recruits, who, like Green, wanted to be part of the football renaissance. Two seasons after Green's graduation, the Orangemen went 11-0-1 and finished fourth in the national rankings. Green wound up winning All-American honors twice while establishing himself as the school's all-time sack leader with 45.5. He was a first-round draft pick of the Atlanta Falcons in 1986 and spent eight seasons in the NFL.

Orange Slice—Dick MacPherson

After Syracuse opened the 1986 football season with four consecutive losses, angry Orange fans formed the "Sack Mac Pack." The only membership requirement was a staunch belief that Orange coach Dick MacPherson should be fired. "Fortunately, my boss [SU athletic director Jake Crouthamel] didn't listen to them," MacPherson said. "Jake was an old football coach, so he could see that we were on the verge of getting this thing turned around. I'll always be grateful to him for sticking his neck out for me."

Members of the soon-to-be-defunct "Sack Mac Pack" wound up being grateful, too. The '86 Orangemen rebounded to win five of their final seven games, setting the table for one of the most unforgettable seasons in Syracuse football history.

The following year the Orangemen went 11-0-1 and wound up number four in the final polls—their highest ranking since the national championship season in 1959. Mac received national coach-of-the-year honors for resurrecting a program that had endured a long dry spell. The native of Old Town, Maine, would guide the Orangemen to five bowl games in ten years, before leaving to coach the NFL's New England Patriots for two seasons.

Blessed with an infectious, fiery personality and boundless energy, MacPherson became so popular in Syracuse that the Onondaga County Republican Party recruited him to run for political office. Though flattered, Coach Mac had no desire to become Mayor Mac. "To be mayor of

Dick MacPherson and the Orangemen erupt after Syracuse took the lead against number-one Nebraska. Winning the national championship in 1959 aside, Syracuse's shocking 17-9 upset over the Cornhuskers in 1984 may be the greatest moment in the program's storied history.

Syracuse, New York would have been a fascinating job, but I realized me and politics would not have been a good match," he said in a New England accent that consistently drops the *r*s. "Even though you know you've made the right decision, you've got to convince a council or other people that it's right. All of a sudden you are not the head coach. You become a mediator, and I don't feel I ever was a good mediator. I wouldn't want to run anything where people run me and tell me how to run my business."

When Frank Maloney resigned following the 1980 season, Crouthamel believed he needed to find a proven coach with a dynamic personality to breathe new life into the program. While working as the head football coach at Dartmouth College in the 1970s, Crouthamel competed against University of Massachusetts teams coached by MacPherson, and the two men struck up a friendship. Mac was coaching linebackers for the Cleveland Browns when Crouthamel came calling. "I saw it as a tough job, but a great opportunity," recalled MacPherson, who became a color commentator on SU football radio broadcasts shortly after his return to Syracuse in 1993. "They were down when I got there and then the university made a big commitment to turn things around."

Success came slowly. After guiding the Orangemen to 4-6-1 and 2-9 records his first two seasons, MacPherson's rebuilding efforts showed signs of life with 6-5 finishes in 1983 and '84 and a 7-5 mark and a Cherry Bowl appearance in '85. But the rotten start the following year convinced many that this would be as good as it gets under MacPherson. "I knew it was going to take some time to make the situation better," he said, "and thank God I had a guy in my corner who was willing to be patient."

In this case, patience was indeed a virtue.

Dick MacPherson

Date of birth: November 4, 1930

Hometown: Old Town, Maine

Honors: 1987 consensus national coach of the year.

Achievements: Was twenty-fifth head football coach in SU history. . . . Led the Orange to five bowl appearances in ten seasons. . . . School's third-winningest football coach behind Ben Schwartzwalder and Paul Pasqualoni. . . . Posted 45-27-1 record at Massachusetts prior to coming to Syracuse. . . . Worked as an assistant in the NFL with the Denver Broncos and Cleveland Browns and on the college level at the Universities of Maryland and Cincinnati. . . . Served as head coach of the New England Patriots from 1991 to 1992.

SU career totals: 66-46-4 coaching record.

14

Get Smart

March 30, 1987   *Five seconds separated Jim Boeheim from*
The Superdome   *his elusive first national championship,*
New Orleans, Louisiana   *but then Indiana's Keith Smart launched a*
jump shot from the left corner, and Syra-
cuse's dream died.

On the evening of the 1987 NCAA basketball championship game, Indiana's Keith Smart couldn't help but think back with a smile to the last time he had been in the New Orleans Superdome. He was a teenager, a Boy Scout hailing from nearby Baton Rouge, Louisiana, and on Sunday afternoons he worked as an usher during New Orleans Saints National Football League games, showing people to their seats. "Way up there by the windows," Smart would say, pointing to the far-away reaches of the stadium.

Smart wasn't showing anyone to their seats on this night as his Hoosiers played Syracuse for the national title. Instead, he brought them out of their seats when he nailed a sixteen-foot jumper from the left corner with five seconds remaining to lift Indiana to a 74-73 victory over the Orangemen, giving Bobby Knight his third championship in eleven years while denying Syracuse's Jim Boeheim his first. "We did not lose the game, Indiana won it," a disconsolate Boeheim said in the aftermath of Syracuse's first appearance in the national championship game. "A loss never feels good, I never coached one that did feel good, but this one hurts more because it's more important than all the rest. But there is only one team better in the country than us, and that's not by much."

There were scores of Syracuse supporters who disagreed on two fronts with Boeheim's assessment. First, they truly believed Syracuse—not Indiana—was the better team. Second, they contended that Indiana did not win so much as Syracuse lost.

It's tough to argue against the evidence. Man for man, Syracuse probably was the better squad, with future NBA players Derrick Coleman, Rony Seikaly, and Sherman Douglas on the roster. And during the final few minutes, the Orangemen had the game in their hands and piddled it away owing to a lack of execution.

With 13 minutes to go Syracuse senior Howard Triche dropped an eighteen-foot jumper that gave the Orange a 52-44 lead, but Indiana proceeded to score the next 10 points, a run that included a three-pointer by Steve Alford (game-high 23 points) and a Smart jumper that put the Hoosiers in front 54-52. Without that surge, Knight said, Indiana probably would not have won the game. "That was a critical point in the ballgame," said Knight. "There was a hell of a lot of time left, but we had brought it back."

The Orangemen responded when Greg Monroe drilled a seventeen-footer and Douglas made two free throws, a three-pointer, and a driving basket to send Syracuse into a 61-56 lead with 7:22 remaining.

Again the Hoosiers rallied, and when Smart banked one in from the right side of the lane, Indiana was back on top, 67-66, with 3:31 to play. That would be the last time the Hoosiers would lead until the final few seconds.

Douglas stole an errant pass by Alford and drove for the go-ahead hoop, and after Indiana's Daryl Thomas tied it with a free throw, Seikaly scored from in close to make it 70-68 with 2:03 to go. Smart's reverse layup tied it, then Triche made a short jumper from the lane with 57 seconds remaining to put the Orangemen back on top 72-70, setting up one of the most exciting finishes in Final Four history.

Smart, who would finish with 21 points to earn Final Four MVP honors, missed a jumper. Triche cleared the rebound and was fouled by Alford with 38 ticks to go. Following a time-out Triche made just one of two free throws, and Smart grabbed the rebound, beat the Orangemen downcourt, and made a twelve-footer to pull the Hoosiers within one, 73-72.

After a time-out, Coleman was quickly fouled with 28 seconds left, and following another time-out, the freshman stepped to the line with a chance to increase the Syracuse lead. Coleman was given a one-and-one rather than a two-shot foul—"I thought it was an intentional foul," Coleman said—and when he missed the front end, Indiana's Thomas yanked the rebound uncontested.

Earlier, with Triche at the line, Boeheim had lined his players up on the lane so they could fight for the rebound, but when Smart pulled it down, he was able to beat Syracuse in transition. Boeheim didn't want that to happen again, so with Coleman at the line, he ordered the rest of the Orangemen to back off and get ready to play defense. "I think I made a mistake [on the Triche miss]," Boeheim admitted. "I think we should have kept guys back. Maybe they wouldn't have gotten the transition basket by Smart."

Of course, Boeheim was then second-guessed for pulling back on the Coleman free throw, but Knight defended his coaching adversary for that decision. "With that time left, he's not going to foul, he's not going to go over somebody's back to get a rebound. The kid misses and then we're going to try to get it out quickly if they've got everybody up there. I think he made the absolute right decision. He's got his defense set. Don't give us a chance to win the game."

Yet Indiana still won the game. When Thomas rebounded Coleman's miss, the Hoosiers did not call time. They brought the ball up and tried to work for the winning shot, but Syracuse—as Boeheim had hoped by keeping his players back—defended stoutly. Indiana wanted Alford to shoot for the win, but Douglas hounded him and denied him the ball.

With the clock dipping inside 10 seconds and 64,959 fans in the Superdome on their feet screaming, Smart forgot about Alford and took the game into his own hands. He dished to Thomas who was posted up on the baseline, then wandered into the corner where Thomas could give it back to him if he couldn't get off a shot. That's what happened. Coleman manned up on Thomas and prevented a shot, so Thomas kicked it out to Smart who let fly just over the outstretched arm of a lunging Triche. "First I want to thank Daryl for not taking the shot and passing the ball back to me," said Smart. "We worked it around and I knew time was running out so I just took the shot. The play was designed for Steve, but it broke down and the shot went to me."

The ball passed through the net with 5 seconds showing on the clock, and then bedlam reigned. Under the basket Seikaly and Coleman, as if paralyzed by the excitement and the noise in the building, did not signal for a time-out, and by the time the officials saw Monroe and Triche calling for one, only 1 second remained.

Boeheim argued madly that Syracuse should have had at least four seconds to orchestrate a winning shot, but the officials did not back down. "It's almost automatic on a made shot like that that if anybody looks like they're calling timeout, you get it," Boeheim said. "It's the officials' job to look for it. But we didn't get it." Douglas, who led Syracuse with 20 points and 7 assists, said: "Maybe we should have called timeout sooner, but maybe we did. The officials should have gone to the monitors and checked in a game like this. But with Indiana and their coach, I don't think they wanted to do that because of the intimidation factor."

Forced to take the ball out under its own basket, Syracuse's plight was hopeless. Coleman's heave was intercepted—fittingly—by Smart, and he proceeded to launch the ball into the air in celebration, leaving Syracuse to wonder what had gone wrong. "I felt confident, I felt comfortable the last 15 minutes," said Monroe. "We were playing good basketball, playing good defense. I thought it looked OK, I thought we were in a good position to win."

Coleman had a huge game with 8 points and 19 rebounds, just two shy of the NCAA Championship record set by Kentucky's Bill Spivey in 1951. But all he could do was lament his missed free throw. "I felt comfortable on the line, but when I released it was off to the right and I knew it as soon as I let go of it," he said. It had been a Syracuse bugaboo all season, poor free throw shooting, and it cost the Orange a national championship. "We had the opportunity to win," said Boeheim. "But we didn't put it away when we had control. If we make either free throw we win the game."

It would take two more opportunities over the next sixteen years before Boeheim and the Orangemen captured that elusive first national championship. In 1996 a far less talented squad than the 1987 team lost 76-67 to Rick Pitino's Kentucky Wildcats. But in 2003, led by Carmelo Anthony and Gerry McNamara, the Orangemen scaled the mountain and defeated Kansas 81-79, appropriately enough in the Superdome where they had suffered such a heartbreaking defeat.

Sherman Douglas took over as point guard when Pearl Washington departed for the NBA, and though not as flashy as the Pearl, Douglas became the all-time NCAA assist king.

Orange Slice—Sherman Douglas

On the March 2003 afternoon when Syracuse University retired his number 20 jersey, Sherman Douglas was asked to compare the current Orange team that had designs on making it to the Final Four with the

1986–1987 team he led not only to the Final Four but to the national championship game as well. "With some of the young guys on the team at that time, it definitely reminds me of how well the '87 team played," Douglas said. "Hopefully they can be a little bit better than the '87 team."

In the end, they were. The 2002–2003 Orangemen took the final step and defeated Kansas in the national championship game. But no one who has played point guard at Syracuse—and that includes Pearl Washington and Gerry McNamara—has ever been better than Douglas.

When Douglas graduated from Syracuse to the NBA in 1989, he was the Orange's all-time leader in points (2,060) and the NCAA's all-time leader in assists (960). More than fifteen years after his departure he remains Syracuse's leader in assists, he ranks second in steals (235) and fourth in scoring, and he still holds the Big East records for assists in a game (22), season (326), and career (426). "Sherman is probably the greatest competitor I have ever coached," said coach Jim Boeheim. "He willed good things to happen. Sherman made himself into a great college basketball player."

Despite leading Spingarn High School to a 31-0 record and a Washington, D.C.–area championship, recruiters were cool toward Douglas, as only Rutgers and Old Dominion showed sincere interest. But when New York City product Boo Harvey, whom Syracuse had targeted to become Washington's replacement, failed to qualify academically, the Orangemen fortuitously reeled in Douglas who—by his own admission—would have been flipping burgers at McDonalds otherwise.

Douglas spent his freshman year backing up Pearl, but when Washington decided to enter the NBA draft after his junior year, Douglas became the starting point guard in 1986–1987. With stars such as Rony Seikaly, Derrick Coleman, and dependable role players like Stevie Thompson, Greg Monroe, and Howard Triche benefiting from Douglas's pinpoint passes, the Orangemen charged all the way to the title game in the New Orleans Superdome where they lost to Indiana on Keith Smart's last-second shot.

During the three years he ran the Syracuse attack, the Orangemen posted a record of 87-24 and won one Big East regular-season title and one Big East Tournament. Individually, Douglas made the 1987 NCAA all-tournament team, was a three-time first-team All–Big East selection, made the Big East all-tournament team three times, and was the tournament MVP in 1988. "He deserved to have his jersey retired," Boeheim said of Douglas, just the fourth player so honored in Orange basketball history. "He had an unbelievable career here."

Sherman Douglas

Date of birth: September 15, 1966

Hometown: Washington, D.C.

Honors: Earned All-American recognition in 1987, '88, and '89. . . . Was national player of the year finalist in 1989. . . . Three-time first-team All–Big East. . . . 1988 Big East Tournament MVP. . . . 1987 NCAA all-tournament team. . . . Number 20 jersey is retired.

Achievements: Still SU's all-time leader in assists (960), a mark that was number one in NCAA history when he left SU. . . . Led SU to 87-24 record during his three years as starting point guard. . . . Averaged 11 points and 6 assists during twelve-year NBA career.

SU career totals: 2,060 points, 960 assists, 235 steals.

15

Take That, Joe Pa

October 17, 1987
Carrier Dome
Syracuse, New York

Not since 1970 had Syracuse beaten Penn State in football, but in the first game between the two schools when both were nationally ranked since 1960, the Orangemen ended their long drought with a resounding Don McPherson–predicted victory.

It was thirteen days before Syracuse quarterback Don McPherson would be playing the most important game to that point in his football career, and while all around him the pressure and the anticipation were already starting to build, McPherson was cooler than the Cardin suits and Dior silk ties he used to wear around campus.

The Orangemen had bolted to a 5-0 start, their best since 1959 when they went 11-0 and won their only national championship. They were ranked thirteenth in the country, and now they had a week off to rest before their fiercest rival, defending national champion Penn State, would be coming to the Carrier Dome for a nationally televised showdown for eastern supremacy.

The hoopla was understandable, but on this day McPherson was oblivious to it all. He had a gut feeling that the tenth-ranked Nittany Lions were ripe for a licking and that the Orangemen were just the team to administer said licking. Even though he was speaking off the record, he had the audacity to predict a monumental Syracuse victory. "It's gonna be a blowout," the senior said. "Their secondary is slow, and the

118

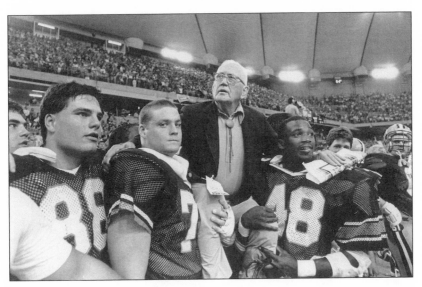

Ben Schwartzwalder gets a celebratory ride off the field after the 1987 team defeated Penn State at the Carrier Dome, ending a seventeen-year drought that extended back to ol' Ben's days on the sidelines.

pass rush won't get to me. We'll throw like crazy and be out ahead by 20 or 25 points."

Wait a minute. This was Penn State McPherson was talking about. A team that had beaten Syracuse senseless for sixteen autumns in a row by an average score of 30-8, including 42-3 the year before, a team that had slain powerful Miami nine months earlier in the Fiesta Bowl to win Joe Paterno's second national title in five years, a team that hadn't endured a losing season in forty-eight years.

The last time Syracuse beat Penn State was in 1970. On that day, Anwar Sadat was sworn in as the third president of Egypt and U.S. aircraft dropped tons' worth of bombs on the Ho Chi Minh Trail. In the sixteen games played since, Penn State had beaten Syracuse by fewer than ten points only twice, had won by at least twenty points on eight occasions, and had blanked the Orangemen in forty of the sixty-four quarters played.

"We'll whip 'em," said McPherson, who had been recruited by Paterno, but not to play quarterback, a slight that McPherson perceived as racist, telling *New York Newsday,* "You can't even picture a black kid in that white helmet lining up behind center at Penn State." Thirteen days later, McPherson stood in a jubilant Syracuse locker room clutching a toy dinosaur in his hand. "That's Godzilla, I watch all his movies; he's my favorite monster," McPherson said, introducing his little companion.

Over the previous three hours, McPherson had been Godzilla, and poor, unsuspecting Penn State was cast in the role of Tokyo during a 48-21 Syracuse demolition that McPherson had foreseen. "Nothing shocked me about this game," McPherson said. "I knew everything that was going to happen. I don't think anything struck us about the way they played us." It was a defeat so complete it moved Paterno—who entered the game with a 19-2 record against Syracuse and an 88-8-1 mark against his main East Coast independent rivals—to say, "They took it easy on us. It could've been a lot worse than it was. I appreciate that."

Syracuse scored on its first play from scrimmage, an 80-yard McPherson bomb to Rob Moore, and the Nittany Lions never recovered. They were down 27-0 at the half and 41-0 midway through the third quarter when Syracuse coach Dick MacPherson decided to start lifting his starters, most prominently McPherson. "I asked him if he wanted to come out and he said 'No, I want to go out there and kick their butts some more,' " Mac said of Mc.

It was such a sweet day for Syracuse and its long-suffering fans, but there was an added touch of redemption for McPherson. When Paterno had come to recruit him, the legendary coach didn't think McPherson could play quarterback. He wanted him to play defensive back. McPherson wanted no part of that experiment, so even though he had dreamed of becoming a Nittany Lion, he chose to attend Syracuse where he knew he'd play quarterback. "When you see them as a kid in the East, they're always the team you want to play for," McPherson said. "And if they're not the team you play for, they become the team you shoot for."

The first time McPherson faced Penn State as a sophomore in 1985, he very nearly ended Syracuse's futility in what used to be one of the East's most storied rivalries. He threw for 173 yards and a touchdown and ran for 56 yards and another score as the Orangemen took a 20-17 lead deep into the fourth quarter. However, with fewer than five minutes to go, fullback Roland Grimes fumbled, Penn State recovered, and

John Shaffer marched the Nittany Lions to the game-winning touchdown, depressing a sellout gathering at the Carrier Dome.

In 1986, McPherson was helpless as Penn State won a 42-3 laugher at State College. But this time it would be different. McPherson knew it. And when Penn State safety Brian Chizmar fell down, allowing Moore to blow by him and haul in McPherson's long pass on the first play, Paterno knew too. "That was just an omen of things to come," Paterno said. "It was an indication of what they could do."

When MacPherson decided to open the game with a bomb, McPherson was thrilled. "Mac came to me on Thursday and said it would be the first play. I loved it, it was beautiful," McPherson said. "That's a break [Chizmar falling and Moore being able to score]. The next thing is our defense goes out and squashes them. Now we're high and they're saying 'This is going to be a ballgame.' "

It was never a ball game. Following the punt, Syracuse drove 42 yards to a 37-yard field goal by Tim Vesling, and after Penn State again failed to make a first down, the Orangemen went 34 yards on its next series to Vesling's 35-yard field goal and a 13-0 lead. After yet another punt, Syracuse scored on its fourth straight possession as McPherson fired a 29-yard touchdown pass to Tommy Kane. The Orangemen had moved to a first-and-goal at the 10, but a delay penalty and losses totaling 14 yards brought up a seemingly hopeless third-and-goal situation from the 29.

If Moore's play didn't signify that this was going to be Syracuse's day, this one did. Kane ran a post pattern into the end zone and was covered well by safety Marques Henderson, but Kane made a terrific leaping catch in the end zone, and it was 20-0.

Penn State finally managed to cross midfield five minutes into the second quarter, but the drive died when Jeff Mangram intercepted a Matt Knizner pass intended for Michael Timpson in the end zone. The teams exchanged punts before the Orangemen marched 70 yards in seven plays to McPherson's six-yard TD run thirty seconds before halftime.

As the teams left the field for intermission, there was little reason for them to bother returning for the final thirty minutes. Penn State entered the game averaging 434.3 yards per game. It had 76 in the first two quarters. Syracuse had 172 yards in the first quarter alone, 301 for the half.

On its first possession of the third, Syracuse continued its relentless attack. It moved 57 yards in eight plays with McPherson hooking up with Kane on another third-and-long touchdown pass, this one a 27-yarder on third-and-18.

Penn State went three-and-out for the fourth time, but a good punt pinned Syracuse deep in its own territory. Facing third-and-8 from the 12, Coach Mac called for a quick kick by fullback Daryl Johnston, and once again the planets were aligned properly for the Orange. The kick caromed off Penn State's Henderson, and Syracuse recovered at the Penn State 20, a 68-yard field-position change. On the next play, McPherson ran the option to perfection and breezed into the end zone to make it 41-0. "That's the best they've run the option against us," Paterno said. "They wouldn't let us get to McPherson from the outside. McPherson got around the corners and we didn't have enough speed to stop him."

Although it was far too late, Penn State came alive briefly when Gary Brown broke free for an 80-yard touchdown run two plays after the kickoff. In the fourth, Penn State's Rich Shonewolf blocked Ken Hawkins's punt and fell on the ball in the end zone for a touchdown, and 2:02 later backup quarterback Tom Bill fired a 59-yard touchdown pass to Ray Roundtree to cut Penn State's deficit to 41-21.

Syracuse slowed the Penn State charge as MacPherson put McPherson back into the game, and a 64-yard pass to Kane resulted in Michael Owens's exclamation-point 1-yard touchdown run with 9 seconds left to wrap up the victory.

One more piece of business needed to be attended to after Owens's score. When Vesling tacked on the extra point, it was Syracuse's 200th consecutive successful point after touchdown, breaking the all-time NCAA record held by Alabama, which had its streak snapped at 199 a month earlier in a victory over Penn State.

McPherson finished with 336 yards passing, a new Syracuse record, and 375 yards of total offense, 9 yards shy of the previous mark set by Bill Hurley during a 31-24 loss to Penn State in 1977. "Total elation," McPherson said. "I am completely happy. It was an extraordinary day in every respect. I did imagine it. I thought the way our defense has been playing, we'd shut them down, and I've felt from the first game we had a high-powered offense."

His performance vaulted him into the national spotlight as a Heisman Trophy candidate, and MacPherson openly campaigned for his quarterback. "I think there are people who can take a look at him now," Coach Mac said. "I don't know anyone out there who is doing for his football team what he is for this team. That's what the Heisman Trophy is all about, isn't it?"

Minutes after the game ended, Paterno ventured over to the Syracuse locker room and praised the Orangemen for their performance. "You're a great team," Paterno told his conquerors. "This was a great win. Keep the national championship in the East."

The Orangemen tried their best, but they came up just short. A thrilling last-second 32-31 victory over West Virginia preserved a perfect 11-0 regular season, and they entered the New Year's Day bowl frenzy ranked fourth in the nation. But a 16-16 tie with Auburn in the Sugar Bowl killed any chances of a title, and Miami clinched the championship when it defeated Oklahoma, 20-14, in the Orange Bowl to conclude its perfect 12-0 season. Syracuse finished fourth in the final AP poll behind Miami, Florida State, and Oklahoma, its highest rank since winning the national title in 1959. The following year, Syracuse went down to State College, and even without the graduated McPherson it beat the Nittany Lions, 24-10, for their first win in Happy Valley since 1970.

Orange Slice—Don McPherson

For three years in the mid-1980s, Don McPherson was quite simply "The Man" around the Syracuse campus. He was the star quarterback who, when he graduated in 1987, was the all-time leading Orange passer with 5,812 yards and who, in 1987, led Syracuse to an 11-0 regular season and an appearance in the New Year's Day Sugar Bowl where Auburn ruined perfection with a 16-16 tie.

But it wasn't until a decade after leaving Syracuse, following an unfulfilling and unsuccessful foray into pro football where he spent three years in the NFL with Philadelphia and Houston and four years with two teams in the Canadian League, when McPherson discovered what being "The Man" was all about. "I had to carry myself in a different way, sometimes not showing emotion, not showing weakness or any kind of

Don McPherson was the runner-up in the 1987 Heisman Trophy balloting as he led Syracuse to an 11-0-1 record and a berth in the Sugar Bowl.

vulnerability," he said of his days as a gridiron great. "It meant being in control all of the time. Most people expected me to be shallow and a womanizer. I struggled with who I really was on the inside versus my need to be a part of the guys who were cool. I realized at the end of my football career that I had to address the other half of myself that I had ignored for so many years. I knew that on the outside I was 'The Man,' but I realized I had to take care of the man inside."

In 1996 McPherson was named director of sport in Society's Mentors in Violence Prevention Program (MVP). A gender violence–prevention program, MVP is designed to encourage men to take a proactive position in the effort to stop men's violence against women. In particular, MVP was designed to address male student athletes and encourage their involvement in campus programs. Through McPherson's efforts, MVP has conducted presentations and programs at more than one hundred high schools, fifty colleges and universities, the New England Patriots training camp, and the NBA's rookie-transition program. "This movement is about challenging what men say to each other in all male environments, how we raise our boys, and how we talk about women which limits who men are," said McPherson, who in 2001 became a member of the Syracuse University Alumni Board and serves on the executive committee and is also involved in a number of other business ventures. "Violence against women is a men's issue and men have to confront other men, otherwise, it won't end."

Not that anyone should be surprised by McPherson's transition from the football field to the business world. During his days at Syracuse McPherson didn't spend time with his teammates in the typical haunts on Marshall Street, and rarely did he partake in the postgame feasts at Grimaldi's. "The Man" was very much his own man, a Renaissance man in many ways. He majored in psychology, wore suits to class, read the *New York Times* daily, and listened to jazz music on his Walkman. "Strange dude," teammate Derek Ward once said of him.

Great player, too. During his magical senior season when he finished runner-up to Notre Dame's Tim Brown in the Heisman Trophy voting, McPherson was the nation's top-ranked passer, edging out UCLA's Troy Aikman, a future number-one-overall draft pick in the NFL. He accounted for 52 percent of Syracuse's total offense with his 2,540 running and passing yards and 62 percent of its scoring with 28 touchdowns (22 passing, 5 rushing, and 1 receiving). When he left the Hill he owned 22 individual records.

Those numbers caught the eyes of other prestigious award voters, and McPherson was a consensus All-American selection and winner of 18 national player of the year honors, including the Maxwell, Davey O'Brien, and Johnny Unitas Awards.

In his role with MVP as well as executive director of the Sports Leadership Institute at Adelphi University, which he founded, McPherson makes dozens of appearances and speeches a year to promote his ideas and challenge the stereotypical image of athletes.

Don McPherson

Date of birth: April 2, 1965

Hometown: Brooklyn, New York

Honors: Was runner-up in 1987 Heisman Trophy balloting and was first-team All-American choice. . . . In 1987 he won Golden Helmet and Maxwell Awards as nation's outstanding player, Davey O'Brien and Johnny Unitas Awards as nation's top quarterback, and ECAC player of the year award. . . . Member of SU's All-Century Team.

Achievements: Holds SU season record for passing efficiency with mark of 164.3. . . . When he graduated he was SU's all-time leader in passing yards with 5,812 yards and total offense with 7,063 yards.

SU career totals: 1,251 rushing yards, 5,812 passing yards, 7,063 total offensive yards, 46 TD passes, 65 TDs total.

16

No Such Thing as a Tie

November 21, 1987   *In what many believe still ranks as the*
Carrier Dome   *most exciting football game ever played at*
Syracuse, New York   *the Dome, the Orangemen came from be-*
hind in the final seconds to defeat West
Virginia and cap a perfect regular season,
their first since the national championship
season of 1959.

When you think of all the marvelous and memorable two-pointers that have been scored in the Carrier Dome in the quarter century of its existence, you can point undeniably to one that stands above all the rest.

No, it was not Pearl Washington's half-court heave at the buzzer to beat Boston College, not a Rony Seikaly slam off an alley-oop pass from Sherman Douglas, not a Derrick Coleman put-back, not a Billy Owens silky-smooth jumper, and not a Carmelo Anthony drive down the lane.

As a matter of fact, the most unforgettable two-pointer ever scored in the Dome didn't even occur in a basketball game. It was Owens's football-playing brother, Michael, scampering around left end into the front corner of the end zone for a two-point conversion with ten seconds left to play that gave the Syracuse gridders a heart-pounding, jaw-dropping 32-31 victory over West Virginia.

That play, which enabled the Orangemen to finish the 1987 regular season with a perfect 11-0 record and secured a berth in the New Year's Day Sugar Bowl, capped what many believe is the most exciting football game ever played on the Hill, be it in the Dome or old Archbold Sta-

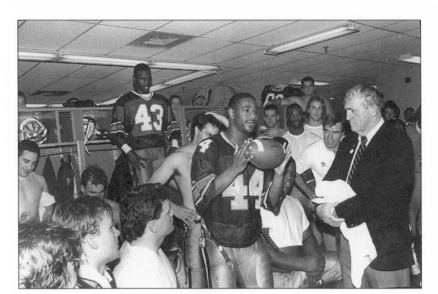

Running back Michael Owens, who scored the deciding two-point conversion in the final seconds of Syracuse's 32-31 victory over West Virginia to cap a perfect 1987 regular season, presents the game ball to coach Dick MacPherson in the jubilant locker room.

dium. "My goodness, I don't believe this," Syracuse safety Markus Paul said after it hit him that Syracuse, a team that had won just 5 of 11 games in 1986, had run the table and was on its way to New Orleans. "It's a miracle," bellowed offensive coordinator George DeLeone amid the bedlam that erupted on the floor of the Dome after the Syracuse defense turned aside a last-ditch West Virginia prayer on the final play of the game. "This is incredible," said quarterback Don McPherson. "When I came here we were 2-9. We would have dreamed to have gone 9-2, let alone 11-0. I'm speechless over all of this."

Syracuse had rolled through its first ten games almost unchallenged, its closest result a 24-13 victory at Missouri back on the first weekend of October. In winning ten straight the Orangemen had risen to number five in the national polls behind Oklahoma, Miami, Florida State, and Nebraska, their highest perch since finishing number one by winning the 1959 national championship.

But here came Don Nehlen's underrated, upset-minded Mountaineers with their brilliant freshman quarterback, Major Harris, looking to spoil Syracuse's perfect season and its outside shot at a national championship. West Virginia battled the Orangemen like no team had in 1987. The 31 points represented one-fifth of the total points Syracuse allowed the entire regular season, and the Mountaineers gained 267 yards on the ground against a defense that had been allowing barely 100 per game.

For the first time all year Syracuse found itself trailing heading into the final quarter, and despite the Orangemen twice rallying to tie the game, the Mountaineers responded each time to regain the lead, the last coming with 1:32 left to play when Undra Johnson scored on a 10-yard run for a 31-24 advantage. But as Syracuse coach Dick MacPherson would say afterward, it wasn't going to be enough, not against this magical Syracuse team. "I think they're still in shock," Coach Mac said of the Mountaineers. "I think they realize they played a team of destiny tonight."

And that destiny rested in the capable hands of McPherson, the All-American who would go on to finish second in the Heisman Trophy balloting behind Notre Dame's Tim Brown.

To this point, it had not been one of McPherson's, or Syracuse's, best days. West Virginia took an early 7-0 lead when John Talley—the brother of former Buffalo Bills great Darryl Talley—caught a 45-yard touchdown pass from Harris one play after Syracuse's Robert Drummond had lost a fumble.

Syracuse went ahead 10-7 on Byron Abraham's 2-yard TD run and Tim Vesling's 30-yard field goal that had been set up by Owens's 30-yard run in the second quarter.

The Mountaineers regained the lead before halftime on Craig Taylor's 1-yard run and Charlie Baumann's 30-yard field goal to cap a monstrous 19-play, 85-yard drive that put West Virginia up 17-10 heading into the final quarter, a 5-touchdown epoch that no Syracuse supporter will ever forget.

Syracuse pulled even when Owens turned a screen pass into a dynamic 65-yard touchdown, only to see Harris hook up with Talley for a 41-yard pass that led to Harris's 3-yard TD run with 10:06 to play. Again Syracuse tied it at 24-24 when fullback Daryl Johnston blew through the middle for a 19-yard touchdown after McPherson hit Tommy Kane for a 30-yard gain to convert a third-and-18.

Undaunted, Harris marched the Mountaineers 67 yards to Johnson's go-ahead touchdown, so back out came McPherson, hoping to once again hold serve. Starting from his own 26 he took the Orangemen on the drive of his life, a drive that should have been enough to convince the Heisman voters that he was the best player in the country in 1987.

McPherson completed a 6-yard pass to Owens, then a 23-yard laser to Deval Glover that put the ball on the West Virginia 45 and brought all 49,866 fans to their feet for the final 57 seconds. After an incompletion, Glover came free again and hauled in a 20-yard pass to the 25, and McPherson called for time-out with 41 ticks remaining. McPherson threw an 8-yard pass to tight end Pat Kelly, and after throwing incomplete toward Johnston, the clock stopped with 15 seconds to go and Syracuse staring at third-and-2 from the 17.

"He looked at me in the huddle and said 'Shake your man, I'm coming to you,'" said Kelly, the late Rochester-area schoolboy star who went on to play briefly in the NFL and died of cancer in 2003. "It's probably the biggest thing anybody has said to me in all my years in athletics." Kelly then went out and made the biggest play in all his years in athletics. "I knew they were double-teaming the wide receivers and playing Pat one-on-one," said McPherson, who before the drive had thrown a career-high 4 interceptions among Syracuse's 6 turnovers. "I knew it was going to be six points at the line of scrimmage."

Kelly ran down the seam, McPherson threw a pass that was a bit high, but the athletic six-foot-five Kelly made an over-the-shoulder grab with West Virginia's Terry White right on his heels, and the Dome literally exploded. However, there was still work to be done, and even as Kelly was thrusting his arms to the heavens in celebration, he knew it. "I was thinking about us needing two points," he said. "I wasn't even thinking about the touchdown."

Syracuse trailed 31-30, and now came the ultimate decision: kick the extra point and preserve an unbeaten season, or go for the two-pointer, preserve an unblemished record, and keep alive the dream of a possible national championship? Coach Mac didn't need the sellout crowd serenading him with "Two! Two! Two!" to make up his mind. "There was never any doubt we were going for it," he said. "I gathered the offense on the sidelines [after West Virginia went ahead on Johnson's TD] and set up what we wanted to do. One of the things I told them was that we were going for two after we scored. We were going for the national championship. I don't think you should do that [kick for a tying extra point]."

Breathing appeared to be optional in the Dome as McPherson brought the Orangemen to the line for the two-point attempt. The entire season was riding on this play, and everyone recognized that. Rarely has the tension been any higher in the building.

"The play was what we call 48-49 load," said Owens, the sophomore who was playing only because Drummond, the starting tailback, had been injured in the third quarter. McPherson was to come to the line, check the defense, then decide which way to run the option. He chose to go left, and as he sprinted down the line he had to either keep the ball or pitch it wide to Owens depending on how the defense reacted. "I wanted the ball, believe me," Owens said. "But I figured Donnie was going in himself in that situation. Then I saw the two guys were going to stop him and I knew I was getting it. I was going to do whatever it took to get that ball in the end zone. I was thinking about 11-0 and when I crossed that goal line I thought 'It's ours.' "

Too bad Auburn coach Pat Dye didn't subscribe to the MacPherson theory that you don't play for a tie. Six weeks later in the Sugar Bowl, with Auburn at the Syracuse 13-yard line and trailing 16-13 in the final seconds, Dye elected to kick a game-tying field goal that ruined the Orange's bid for a perfect 12-0 season, not to mention preventing Auburn from possibly winning the game. MacPherson was livid because he felt Dye should have gone for a winning touchdown. "I would not have gone for the tie," Coach Mac fumed. "I don't like ties." The tie did not affect Syracuse's bid for the national championship because Miami defeated Oklahoma in the Orange Bowl to win the title, and the Orangemen finished fourth in the final polls.

Orange Slice—Pat Kelly

There was no greater moment in Pat Kelly's football career at Syracuse than the night he caught Don McPherson's touchdown pass in the final seconds against West Virginia to give Syracuse a chance to complete a perfect 1987 regular season. But that catch, and that monumentally exciting victory, meant so little in comparison to the moment Kelly en-

The late Pat Kelly, who died of cancer in 2003, poses at the Dome in 2002 after receiving the Mike and Judy Zunic Courage Award. From left to right are Chancellor Kenneth Shaw, unidentified woman, Pat Kelly, Kari Kelly holding baby Patrick Kelly, Tim Ahern, and Jake Crouthamel.

joyed nearly fifteen years later on the evening of September 7, 2002, when he and his wife, Kari, walked to midfield at the Carrier Dome to accept the Mike and Judy Zunic Courage Award.

On New Year's Day 2001, Kelly was diagnosed with brain cancer and was given six months to live. In typical Kelly fashion, he refused to give in to the insidious disease, underwent high-risk surgery, and there he was, nearly a year after he was supposed to have been dead, smiling and waving to the appreciative crowd at the Dome. "It would have been ridiculous not to have attacked this thing the way we have," said Kelly. "I was 36 and I had a wonderful wife who I wanted to grow old with and a little boy who I wanted to see play football and go to college and get married. I had too much to live for to just go home and die."

However, less than a year later, in April 2003, Kelly did die. Doctors removed 98 percent of his brain tumor in surgery while the final 2 percent was eradicated by chemotherapy in the spring of 2001, and it looked as if Kelly was going to be one of the lucky ones, a cancer survivor. But shortly after that night in the Dome when the former tight end and his wife were given the Zunic Award—presented annually in memory of the former SU linebacker and his wife who sacrificed their lives while saving the lives of others in a 1989 plane crash in Sioux City, Iowa—he learned that the cancer had returned. Kelly died at his home in Charlottesville, Virginia, at the age of thirty-seven.

Kelly was one of the finest athletes to hail from Rochester. At Webster Thomas High School he was an All–Greater Rochester football quarterback, a six-foot-five basketball center/forward on a 23-1 team that won a Section V Championship, and a star lacrosse midfielder. He was elected to the Section V Football Hall of Fame in 1998.

At Syracuse Kelly was a two-year letter winner who caught 44 passes for 631 yards and 4 TDs, and his blocking skills prompted the Denver Broncos to choose him in the seventh round of the 1988 NFL draft. "Who would've guessed that a high school quarterback would become a pro prospect at tight end," said Orange coach Dick MacPherson who recruited Kelly. "It's a credit to him."

Kelly played two years for the Broncos and two years for the New York Jets, primarily as a special teams player, before retiring to Wall Street where he put his education to use and became director of equity trading for the Bear Stearns Company, Inc.

Syracuse fans will never forget his touchdown catch against the Mountaineers. Nor will they forget the courage he showed when confronted with the greatest battle of his much-too-short life.

Pat Kelly

Date of birth: October 29, 1965

Hometown: Rochester, New York

Honors: Mike and Judy Zunic Courage Award, 2002.

Achievements: Made one of the most memorable catches in school history, a 17-yard TD reception with ten seconds remaining that helped SU defeat West Virginia and preserve a perfect 11-0 regular season. . . . Played four years in the NFL before retiring in 1991.

SU career totals: 44 receptions, 631 yards, 4 TDs.

17

Air Gait Takes Flight

May 30, 1988
Carrier Dome
Syracuse, New York

The Orangemen have won nine national championships in lacrosse, an unprecedented run that began in 1983. But it was their 1988 victory—which came at the expense of Upstate New York rival Cornell—that jump-started the Syracuse dynasty as we know it today.

The list of players who have played lacrosse at Syracuse reads like the sport's Hall of Fame ballot. It starts with the great Jim Brown and is connected through the eras by the likes of Tim O'Hara, Brad Kotz, Tim Nelson, John Zulberti, Gary Gait, Paul Gait, Tom Marechek, Charlie Lockwood, Casey Powell, Ryan Powell, and Michael Powell, to name just a few. If Syracuse were to hold an alumni game, it would be akin to Old Timers Day at Yankee Stadium. We're talking the elite of the elite, which explains why the Orangemen qualified for the NCAA Division I Final Four an unfathomable twenty-two consecutive years between 1983 and 2004 and won the crown a record nine times.

But in 1988 when Syracuse captured its second national title of the modern NCAA Tournament era that began in 1971—a team that featured the incomparable Gait brothers—it was a group of players that not even the sport's most devoted fans would remember today who played the key role. Their names were Pat McCabe, Mark Stopher, Jim McNamara—who all play the less glamorous position of long stick defense—and goalie Matt Palumb who put the clamps on Cornell and led the Orangemen to a 13-8 victory at the Carrier Dome in front of 20,220 parti-

134

Twin brothers Paul Gait (19) and Gary Gait (22) revolutionized the game of field lacrosse when they came down from Canada to play for Syracuse. The Orangemen won three straight national championships during the Gait era.

san spectators, then the largest crowd in NCAA lacrosse history. "I bet you can't tell me all of my kids' names on defense," Orange coach Roy Simmons Jr. asked the assembled media following the first and still only Division I lacrosse championship game between New York State–based schools. "Imagine our unsung defense holding Cornell to one goal in 30

minutes. That first-half was unbelievable. Yeah, we have superstars."
On this day, he wasn't talking about the Gaits.

That's not to say the brothers had nothing to do with Syracuse's
romp through the Big Red, nor the other fourteen games—all of which
top-ranked Syracuse won—during the regular season and NCAA Tournament. Gary Gait, who scored the first two goals against Cornell, set
NCAA single-season records in 1988 with fourteen goals in the tournament and seventy goals overall. And two days before the title game in
the semifinals against Pennsylvania, he invented a new move that was
later outlawed. Twice Gait leaped from behind the net and dunked the
ball under the crossbar to help lift the Orangemen to an 11-10 victory.
"He did something no one has seen before," said Simmons of the play
that came to be known as Air Gait. "Watching that shot was like being
there the first time someone slam-dunked a basketball." Said Penn
goalie John Kanaras: "I don't know what the hell he was doing. I was
amazed."

McCabe, a freshman on that 1988 team who would end up winning three national championships at SU and earning first-team All-
American recognition three times, remembered being dumbfounded
when he saw Gait flying from behind the cage. "Everybody looked at
each other," McCabe said. "We weren't really surprised, but at the same
time nothing could have surprised us anymore with him. We're standing there wondering 'Is it legal, is it going to count?' Even the officials
weren't sure."

Not to be outdone, Gary's identical twin, Paul, scored forty-seven
goals in 1988, including one with three seconds remaining that delivered the victory against Penn.

But against the Big Red—the surprise team of the year after rebounding from a 2-5 start with seven consecutive wins to reach the championship—it was the unheralded Syracuse defense that stole the show.

Syracuse opened an early 2-1 lead, then lost Zulberti to a sprained
shoulder. With its best attackman (the Gaits were both midfielders) out
for the day and the Gaits being handled reasonably well by the Cornell
defense, Palumb and his fellow Orange defenders had to step up, and
they did. "Our other guys had to take over," said defensive middie Bill
Dirrigl. Neil Alt, who along with Dirrigl served as a cocaptain of this
team, agreed: "We showed people our defense is just as good as our
offense."

It was hard to tell who was better through the first two and a half quarters. SU jumped to a 10-1 lead as the offense worked hard to beat Cornell goalie Paul Schimoler—who was coming off a marvelous performance in the Big Red's 17-6 semifinal rout of Virginia—and the defense was impenetrable. Gary Gait scored the first two goals, then Brook Chase (twice), Rodney Dumpson, Greg Burns, and Keith Owens beat Schimoler before Paul Gait gave SU an 8-1 halftime lead. Jim Egan and Burns scored early in the third quarter to make it 10-1, and it looked like Cornell—who had beaten Syracuse 18-15 in the national semifinals a year earlier at Rutgers University—was never going to score again.

But Richie Moran, the longtime Cornell coach who had guided the Big Red to three national championships in the 1970s, called this "one of the greatest comeback Cornell teams," and he was proven correct as Cornell responded with four in a row to pull to 10-5.

That's when the Orangemen regained their defensive dominance. Dirrigl won the face-off following Cornell's fifth goal and fed Burns who raced in and scored 47 seconds before the end of the third quarter. With the Dome rocking, Simmons knew that goal was the dagger in Cornell's Big Red heart and he said afterward: "It wasn't a case of 'if' we were going to win the national championship, but how much the cushion would be." It turned out to be 5 as the defense kept the Big Red away from Palumb—who made a career-best 21 saves to win game MVP honors—for most of the rest of the afternoon.

McCabe remembers the 1988 championship because that one kick-started a dynasty, as Syracuse won again in 1989 and 1990. "I don't know if you ever will see that again," McCabe said in reference to the talent level that roamed the Dome during the Gait era. "I look back and I feel very fortunate to have been involved in that. It was all timing, I got there at the right time and was fortunate to be part of the history of the game. We expected to win, and once we got over the hump and won the first one, and we added guys who improved the team, we had a cockiness to us, a confidence to us. We knew if we played our game we were going to win."

When the Orangemen lost the national championship game in 1984 and '85, then were eliminated in the semifinals in '86 and '87, there were some in the lacrosse community who thought Syracuse was annually overrated and couldn't win the big one. But that talk ended promptly when Syracuse reeled off

Gary Gait pulls off the remarkable Air Gait maneuver against Pennsylvania in the national semifinal game at the Carrier Dome in 1988.

its three consecutive titles from 1988 to 1990, then piled on five more championships in 1993, 1995, 2000, 2002, and 2004. Its nine championships are the new Division I standard.

Orange Slice—The Gait Brothers

It was during the pinnacle of their days at Syracuse, the 1990 season, when Gary Gait and Paul Gait and the rest of the Orangemen dominated college lacrosse the way no team ever had or ever has, when coach Roy Simmons Jr. truly came to understand how special the identical twins were. "It's like having Magic Johnson, only there's two of him," Simmons said.

Gary and Paul. Paul and Gary. The Gait brothers revolutionized the game when they came down from British Columbia, Canada, in 1987 to play for the Orangemen, and lacrosse's explosion in popularity over the past decade is directly attributable to their influence.

"There's no question that's a part of history for me," Gary said of his days at Syracuse when the Orangemen won fifty-one of the fifty-six games he and Paul played, including their last twenty-seven, and captured three straight NCAA championships. "It opened up the door for me to stay down in the U.S. and involve myself in lacrosse, entrench myself in the game, and help to grow it," Gary continued. "Here I am years later [he and Paul turned thirty-eight in April 2005] still having that opportunity and it's exciting and it's because of those years in Syracuse. That was the beginning."

Prior to their arrival on campus, Syracuse was still merely an up-and-coming power. It had won its first national championship in 1983, but lost in the next two title games and then in the national semifinals in 1986. As freshmen, Gary and Paul led the Orangemen to a 9-4 record, but they were again eliminated in the semifinals, 18-15, by Cornell.

However, starting in 1988, the Gaits lorded over a dynasty, as Syracuse won forty-two of forty-three games and three straight titles. The two midfielders earned first-team All-American honors their last three years, and Gary remains the all-time record holder for goals in a game (9, tied with Casey Powell and Greg Tarbell), season (70), and career (192). "I think we started a great tradition there," Gary said. "Now when you think of college lacrosse, you think of Syracuse."

From "Air Gait" to the "Backbreaker" to the "Alley-Oop" and all the other behind-the-back and through-the-legs passes and shots in between, the Gaits became the Harlem Globetrotters of lacrosse, a true "Gait" attraction, if you will. Before the Gaits, attendance at Syracuse lacrosse games was sparse, usually a few hundred fans out at Coyne Field, later a few thousand when the Carrier Dome opened and Final Four appearances became commonplace. During 1990, the final year of the Gait era, the average home attendance was 11,640.

"I came on campus as a freshman [in 1988] and everyone was talking about them," said former SU defender Pat McCabe. "How good can these guys be? We get out there on the first day and you realize how exceptional they were. They were such an unusual package of everything. You saw big guys, fast guys, guys who handled the stick well, but never did you see guys that were the total package of size, speed, intelligence and flair like they were."

From Syracuse they went on to star in professional indoor lacrosse. Gary retired in 2005 after a fifteen-year career that saw him score more than 600 goals and 1,000 points, win six league MVP awards, earn All-Pro honors every year, and play on five championship teams. Paul called it quits in 2002 after more than 400 goals, 700 points, eleven All-Pro selections, and three championships.

The Powell brothers—Casey, Ryan, and Mike—have certainly left an indelible mark on Syracuse, and lacrosse. The incomparable Jim Brown, a Pro Football Hall of Famer considered by many to be the greatest football player ever, is also regarded by those who saw him play lacrosse at Syracuse as the game's greatest player. But in the end, it is the Gaits. No one was better, and no one has had an impact on the game like the Gait twins.

So who was the best? Tom Marechek, another Canadian native who joined the Gaits at Syracuse in 1989, was asked that by a fan in a chat room one time. "That question is a tough one," Marechek answered, "because just when you think one is better, the other one scores seven on you."

Gary Gait

Date of birth: April 5, 1967

Hometown: Victoria, British Columbia

Honors: Four-time All-American (three first-team honors). . . . 1990 NCAA Tournament MVP. . . . Member of NCAA's twenty-fifth-anniversary team selected in 1997. . . . Two-time NCAA player of the year and two-time midfielder of the year.

Achievements: Scored 192 goals, which is SU's all-time record and just 1 shy of all-time NCAA record. . . . Still holds NCAA Tournament records for career goals (50) and points (65) and goals (15) and points (23) in one tournament. . . . Played pro indoor lacrosse for fifteen years and was six-time league MVP.

SU career totals: 192 goals, 61 assists, 253 points.

Paul Gait

Date of birth: April 5, 1967

Hometown: Victoria, British Columbia

Honors: Three-time first-team All-America selection. . . . 1989 NCAA Tournament MVP. . . . Member of NCAA's twenty-fifth-anniversary team selected in 1997.

Achievements: Scored 27 goals and 45 points in NCAA Tournament games. . . . Played pro indoor lacrosse for twelve years. . . . Played for Team Canada four times in World Lacrosse Championship Tournament.

SU career totals: 127 goals, 85 assists, 212 points.

18

A Dynasty Takes Shape

May 29, 1989
Byrd Stadium
College Park, Maryland

With Gary Gait and Paul Gait blowing up scoreboards up and down the eastern seaboard, offense was the name of the game for the Orangemen, but their victory in the 1989 national championship game over Johns Hopkins was a product of stout defense at the most opportune moment.

They were a team that prided itself on playing at a breakneck pace on offense, up and down the field, salivating when an opportunity for transition presented itself, laughing as they watched helpless defenders trying to keep pace. It was run, run, run; shoot, shoot, shoot; and score, score, score for the Orangemen during that glorious epoch in the late 1980s and early 1990s when Syracuse dominated the college lacrosse world, winning three straight national championships. "Most Syracuse games, if you look at them, the other team usually has the possession time," midfielder Rodney Dumpson once said. "We just run and gun. With us it's basically one or two passes and then somebody shoots. Once we get possession of the ball, there's no telling what we can do." It was easy for the Orangemen to play that style with high scorers such as Gary Gait, Paul Gait, Tom Marechek, John Zulberti, and Greg Burns filling opposing nets with alarming regularity.

But when the moment of truth arrived in the 1989 championship game on the campus of the University of Maryland, it was the Syracuse defense—so often relegated to supporting-role status—that sealed a thrilling 13-12 victory over Johns Hopkins. "I want to go on record as

During the late 1980s and early 1990s Syracuse was virtually untouchable on the lacrosse field. Roy Simmons Jr.'s 1990 national championship team, which featured Paul Gait, Tom Marechek, and Gary Gait, is considered one of the best in the sport's history.

saying Matt Palumb is the most underrated goalie I've ever seen play the game," said Pat McCabe, who played long-stick defense for the Orangemen from 1988 to 1991, and thus he held aloft the coveted Division I championship plaque three times. "He doesn't get nearly the credit he should have. It was very easy to overlook our end of the field, and, to some extent how great Matt was. He was a great communicator, he was big in the locker room, and as much as he was a teammate and leader, he was a fan of everyone."

And everyone wearing orange among the crowd of 23,893 sun-soaked spectators at Byrd Stadium on that glorious Memorial Day became a big fan of Palumb when he stopped a point-blank shot by John Hopkins's John Wilkens with one second remaining to preserve the middle championship of that three-year dynasty. "I just remember that it was a great game, and to win it by one goal and to have them have a shot with no time left and Matt Palumb to make a big save, it was a great game," said Gary Gait, the goal-scoring machine who, despite the procession of Powell brothers who have passed through the Carrier Dome the past decade, still holds the school career record for goals with 192.

Coming off its championship in 1988, Syracuse was ranked number one at the start of 1989, but it went down to Baltimore to open the season against Johns Hopkins and the Blue Jays pulled out a 14-13 victory. That day, Syracuse midfielder Steve Scaramuzzino remembered thinking what comes around goes around as he watched the Blue Jays celebrate their victory. Scaramuzzino's thought was "Let them laugh now, we'll see them again."

In the moments after Syracuse gained the ultimate revenge, Scaramuzzino said, "I guess that was kind of a smart-aleck remark, but I knew if we saw them again we'd redeem ourselves. This one was for all the marbles, and that's the bottom line."

Since losing to Hopkins 11-4 in the 1985 title game at Providence, Syracuse had played the storied Blue Jays four times and three of the games were decided by a single goal. Syracuse had won 11-10 in 1986, 15-14 in '87, and 19-7 in '88 before losing the '89 opener. "We always looked at the Hopkins game as a huge game," said McCabe. "Once we started practice we would count down the days to when we played them. It hurt that we lost that first game that year, but coach Simmons always used to say 'It's more important where you are in May than where you are in March.' "

Syracuse responded to that defeat by winning its final 11 regular-season games, and when May rolled around the Orangemen had regained the number-one ranking and earned the top seed in the NCAA Tournament.

Routs over Navy (18-11) and Maryland (18-8 on the Terrapins' home field in the semifinals) sent Syracuse flying into the final where the Orangemen were confronted with an 11-1 Hopkins team that had dispatched Massachusetts (9-4) and North Carolina (10-6) in the quarters and semis. "A lot of people felt that this could have been a one-sided game and that Syracuse had too much firepower for any team," Johns Hopkins coach Don Zimmerman said. "They're so good in transition that if one little thing goes wrong underneath, they can score. They have tremendous shooters."

But Syracuse also had tremendous defenders, and when the Blue Jays' Dave Pietramala—one of the finest long-stick defensemen in history—managed to shut down Gary Gait, holding him to two goals, and the other Syracuse shooters struggled to find holes in All-American goalie Quint Kessenich's armor, Syracuse had to rely on its own goal preventers to survive. "One thing I remember is the game never got in anyone's favor, it was even throughout," McCabe said, referring to the seven ties and seven lead changes that took place. "It was one of those games where we were confident but never comfortable. We knew it was going to come down to the end and we were hoping we'd be in the lead when it ended." And they were, thanks in large part to McCabe and Palumb.

The Blue Jays jumped out to a 4-2 lead, but Syracuse answered with a three-goal run to move ahead by the end of the first quarter. Back came Hopkins, as Wilkens tied the game early in the second on a man-up goal, and Matt Panetta—McCabe's former teammate at Elmont High School on Long Island and Hopkins's prime offensive weapon—scored two in a row. When Greg Kelly won the face-off after Panetta's second goal, scooped the loose ball and went all the way to the cage to beat Palumb, Johns Hopkins was ahead 8-5 and Syracuse coach Roy Simmons was signaling for a time-out.

Paul Gait, who had scored Syracuse's first three goals, notched his fourth to cut the Hopkins lead to 8-6 at halftime, and then Syracuse pulled even early in the third. Palumb stuffed John Dressel from in close, the rebound ricocheted out to Paul Gait, and he started a fast break that ended with him feeding Burns for a goal at 1:30. Then Mike

Magee, whom Simmons used in place of Kirk Pratt on face-offs in the second half, won the ensuing draw. After showing uncharacteristic patience on offense, the Orangemen got the equalizer when Joe Bonacci fired a long shot through Kessenich.

Johns Hopkins scored three of the next four to make it 11-9 heading into the fourth, but it could not hold off the Orangemen in the final 15 minutes. Burns fed Dumpson 10 yards in front of the net, and he whipped one past Kessenich at 2:31, and then Gary Gait tied it from just outside the crease.

Zulberti, who had played only briefly in the title game victory over Cornell the previous year before exiting with a shoulder injury, put the Orangemen ahead for good when he dove from the side and stuffed one in. And then Dumpson gave Syracuse its first two-goal lead of the day when he converted a perfect pass from Paul Gait. "I knew the double team was coming on Paul or Gary, so I tried to find a seam and put myself there," said Dumpson, the always-overlooked man on the first midfield that included the Gait brothers. "I was hoping the ball would come to me, and fortunately, it did. I tucked it in and let it go. I mean, I let it fly."

Wilkens pulled Hopkins to 13-12 with 2:03 remaining, but then Magee won the face-off and Syracuse managed to whittle all but 12 seconds off the clock before Pietramala stripped Gary Gait of the ball and Zimmerman called for a quick time-out.

Zimmerman set up a play for Panetta, who already had five goals in the game, to isolate and go to the net. Simmons stuck to his plan and kept McCabe in coverage on Panetta. It was All-American against All-American. "Pat is a great takeaway checker, but sometimes he is overaggressive," Panetta said. "If you can hide your stick well you can beat him, but he got the better of me today."

On the restart Panetta tried to drive from the right wing, but McCabe cut him off beautifully and forced him to pass behind the net to Jeff Ihm. Ihm quickly spotted a hole in the Syracuse defense. Wilkens saw the same thing and ran toward the net where Ihm hit him with a perfect pass. Now it was Wilkens against Palumb, one-on-one, with the clock racing toward zero. Wilkens took a look and fired, and he hit Palumb right in the chest, the ball falling to the ground as the horn sounded to end the game. "I made myself as wide as I could and I caught it with my chest," said Palumb. "It was great strategy on both sides. They gave it to their best player [Panetta] and we put our best defenseman on him [McCabe] and luckily we made the play."

Simmons, looking as calm as ever on the sidelines during the frantic finish, revealed afterward that he had no doubt his defense would stand tall.

> I talked to Matt during the timeout and I told him when the game ends the ball would be in his stick and we would have the gold trophy. The ball fell out of his stick, but we still have the gold.
>
> It was a great team effort to come from behind in a hot stadium and in a pressure-filled situation. We came to the tournament highly favored which is not the most comfortable position to be in. But when it came down to Memorial Day, we were there and when that big trophy came out, they gave it to us.
>
> The kids had to suck it up and not walk away with a lifelong memory of letting a championship get away. Back-to-back championships are hard to come by, but the players did what they had to do and now they have two gold rings.

Some of those players received a third gold ring the following year when Syracuse made it three championships in a row, capping off an undefeated 1990 season with a 21-9 blowout over Loyola in the final at Rutgers. "Out of the four years I was there, the '90 team was definitely the best," said Gary Gait. "The '89 team was great to only have that one loss in the first game and come back and not lose another game; that's the sign of a great team. But that '90 team, that was total domination of college lacrosse. We blew out everyone that year."

Orange Slice—Tom Marechek

In the 1988 NCAA Lacrosse Tournament, Orange fans were treated to perhaps the most creative goal in the game's history when Gary Gait leaped from behind the cage and dunked the ball under the crossbar at the Carrier Dome against Penn. That maneuver, now banned by the game's rule book, will forever be known as Air Gait.

No one came up with a nifty moniker for the goal Tom Marechek scored a year later in the 1989 tournament, also at the Carrier Dome, this time against Navy, but it certainly deserved one. "I caught a pass from

Greg Burns and had plenty of time in front of the net, so I faked—two, three, four, and then five times and put my hands up in the air like I had already shot and scored," Marechek recalled. "The goalie then turned backwards to scoop the ball out of the goal and then I shot it in." Looking back on that moment during his freshman season at Syracuse, Marechek isn't exactly proud of the fact that he embarrassed the Navy goalie, but sometimes when you have so much talent at your disposal, it's hard not to show it off.

The brothers Gait (Gary and Paul) and the brothers Powell (Casey, Ryan, and Mike) are widely considered to be the most dominant offensive players in Syracuse's proud lacrosse history, but no one should overlook the accomplishments of Marechek.

Gary Gait is the school's all-time leading goal scorer with 192. Who ranks second? Not Paul. Not any of the Powells. It's Marechek, with 182. Further, his 258 career points rank seventh all-time, ahead of both of the Gait brothers, and his 53-goal season in 1991 is the fourth best in school history, a number none of the Powells ever achieved. "If you left him alone, he made you pay," said his old Syracuse teammate defenseman Pat McCabe. "He never forced anything, just let the game come to him."

Coach Roy Simmons found the Gaits in Canada, an unusual recruiting strategy considering most Canadian boys grew up playing indoor box lacrosse and rarely excelled in the field game. The Gaits were an obvious exception. So, too, was Marechek. "We don't have too much high school lacrosse in Canada, so I basically grew up playing box lacrosse and some field on club teams," he said. "I still remember when I was young, coming home from school all excited about the lacrosse game I had that evening. That's the normal way a young Canadian lacrosse player starts his childhood career. I think the better players in Canada took that extra time to improve on their own."

The Gaits knew of Marechek from box lacrosse, and they told Simmons about him. Marechek had been out of high school for more than a year and was trying to get his grades up to an acceptable college standard. Once he did, Simmons came calling with a scholarship, despite never having seen him play and relying solely on the word of the Gait boys that Marechek was a great player.

Marechek helped SU win a pair of national championships and he earned first-team All-American honors three years in a row. "I worked hard to get my grades up, taking a few classes at home after I had graduated," said Marechek, who has played twelve spectacular years of pro indoor lacrosse in the National Lacrosse League. "Then, Paul and Gary told coach Simmons that I was ready to go to college and the rest is history."

Tom Marechek

Date of birth: August 25, 1968

Hometown: Kitchener, Ontario

Honors: Four-time All-American (three first-team selections).

Achievements: Ranks second on SU's all-time goal-scoring list behind only Gary Gait. . . . Scored 30 goals and 46 points in NCAA Tournament games. . . . Has played pro indoor lacrosse for twelve years and also played for Team Canada in World Lacrosse Championships three times.

SU career totals: 182 goals, 76 assists, 258 points.

19

Hoya Paranoia Boils Over

March 4, 1990
Carrier Dome
Syracuse, New York

An editorial in the Georgetown campus newspaper, the Hoya, *once proclaimed that "rooting against Syracuse is as easy as rooting against some sort of horrible disease." That about explains the fervor of the Syracuse-Georgetown rivalry, and it was never hotter than the 1990 afternoon when Hoya coach John Thompson blew his stack and Syracuse went on to a thrilling overtime victory.*

They call it March Madness for a reason, but the madness that is the college basketball season in March arrived a bit early in 1990 for fierce Big East rivals Syracuse and Georgetown.

And nobody was madder than Hoyas coach John Thompson after Syracuse had completed a season sweep of his team—a first since the formation of the Big East eleven years earlier—with a heart-pounding 89-87 victory at the raucous Carrier Dome.

First there was his titanic meltdown late in the first half when he was ejected from the game after being assessed three consecutive technical fouls, which allowed the Orangemen to produce what, in effect, was an unheard-of game-changing ten-point possession.

Then, with Thompson watching the television in the Georgetown locker room and preparing to greet his victorious players as they charged in, Hoyas forward Sam Jefferson committed one of the dumbest fouls in school history. He pushed Syracuse's Billy Owens at mid-court, and instead of having to attempt a half-court prayer, Owens was awarded a trip to the free-throw line with one second remaining, and he made both shots to send the game into overtime.

Finally, Thompson was surely beside himself when his defense, in its eagerness to double-team Syracuse's Derrick Coleman, left Stephen Thompson wide open underneath the basket with twenty-five seconds left in overtime. Coleman made a nifty pass, and Stevie caught it and laid the ball in, giving the Orangemen an 89-86 lead that Georgetown could not overcome.

"With all the ups and down, it was kind of storybook, you know," Coleman said of Syracuse's victory in front of 33,015 crazies, which stands today as the second-largest on-campus crowd in NCAA basketball history. The win gave the Orangemen a share of the Big East regular-season championship with Connecticut and the number-one seed in the Big East tournament and prevented the hated Hoyas from doing the same. "I think Georgetown played as well as I've seen a Georgetown team play," said Syracuse coach Jim Boeheim. "They played great because we played great the whole way." Yet had it not been for Georgetown's mental lapses, Syracuse would not have won the final home game of Coleman's and Stephen Thompson's careers.

There have been so many juicy matchups between these two schools through the years, but this was certainly one of the most delectable. Georgetown was led by the imposing twin towers Dikembe Mutombo and Alonzo Mourning, augmented by Jefferson, Dwayne Bryant, and Mark Tillmon. Syracuse countered with one of its best teams—Coleman, Thompson, Owens, LeRon Ellis, and Michael Edwards.

Just more than a month earlier the Orangemen had gone into the Capital Centre and played one of the best games any Boeheim team had ever played, blowing out Georgetown 95-76, behind 36 points by Owens. That day John Thompson had said to the Orangemen, "Just wait," meaning he would have his Hoyas in an ornery, revenge-seeking mood for the rematch at the Dome. And sure enough, the Hoyas came to Syracuse on a roll, ranked seventh in the country with a 22-4 record, 11-4 in the conference. Syracuse entered 21-5 and 11-4, ranked tenth, and not the least bit intimidated.

The game was played at a brisk early pace, and Georgetown had the better of it as 13 minutes into the first half the Hoyas were ahead 32-22. Then came Thompson's tirade.

Syracuse had rallied to within 36-33 when Bryant stripped Coleman but was called for a reach-in foul with 2:14 to go. Thompson leaped from his chair and began railing against officials Jim Burr, Larry Lembo, and Pete Pavia. Although Pavia made the original call, it was Burr whom Thompson berated, and after Coleman made the first free throw, Burr slapped Thompson with the first technical. That only enraged Thompson further, and in rapid succession he was T'd up by Lembo and then by Pavia, ending his day on the sidelines. With the Dome rocking in derision, Thompson stalked off the court with his arms raised above his head, inciting the crowd to make more noise.

Once Thompson had dramatically exited, Coleman settled in for a lengthy stint at the line. The senior forward—who would ultimately score 27 points for the second-best total of his career—completed the second half of his original foul. He then made five of the six technical-foul free throws, drawing a louder cheer every time the scoreboard clicked an additional point. When Coleman was done, Syracuse had gone from down 36-33 to ahead 40-36. And the Orangemen weren't through. They still owned possession, and after inbounding, Owens drained a three-pointer for a 43-36 lead.

A 10-point run without Georgetown ever touching the ball. There was much more basketball to be played, but this sequence proved critical to the outcome. "John Thompson helped us," Owens said. "We were down, they had the momentum. We had some doubt." Thompson owned up to the blunder, saying, "I probably let my competitive juices overflow. It probably was my fault more than the officials' fault. I made a mistake. But I expected to win the game. I respect all three of those men and have worked with them before. It happens. In competition it happens."

Syracuse took a 45-40 lead into the break and stretched that advantage to 7 points on three occasions in the second half, the last at 69-62 with 7:56 to play.

But the Hoyas would not go away. With Mourning on the bench in foul trouble, Mutombo (19 points, 12 rebounds, 5 blocked shots) became a force inside, and the rest of the Hoyas played aggressive defense that took Syracuse out of its fast break. "You either go down with the pressure or you step up and play," said Bryant, who totaled a career-best 25 points and 9 assists. "I thought we did a very good job of stepping up and playing." They did such a good job that when Mourning converted a three-point play with 2:32 left, the Hoyas were back in the lead for the first time since Thompson's departure at 79-78.

After some fierce back-and-forth play produced no points, the Orangemen drew even when Coleman, fouled by Mutombo on a put-back, made one of two free throws with 28 seconds remaining.

Georgetown patiently played for the last shot, and Mourning was supposed to take it, but he never got the chance, as Ellis fouled him with 4 seconds to go. When he made both shots for an 81-79 lead, things looked bleak for the Orange. However, that's when Jefferson committed a major mistake, bumping Owens near midcourt. "I was just trying to put pressure on him," Jefferson said. "The ref called it, so I guess it was a foul."

"I was kind of surprised," said Owens, who scored 16 of his 23 points during the final 16 minutes of the game. "He was on my hip and riding me. I was just trying to lean into him and make it seem like he was messing me up. If he didn't foul me, I was putting it up." With the crowd in a nervously hushed state, Owens sank both shots to force the overtime. Was the super sophomore nervous? "I don't get nervous about anything," said Owens. "I just tried to concentrate on the rim. It's only me and the rim. In that situation the rim is my only enemy. I just wanted to beat the rim."

In the overtime Owens scored a pair of baskets to give Syracuse an 85-83 lead, and after Bryant tied it with two free throws, Coleman hit a shot from the lane. Then Mourning made a free throw with 1:04 left to pull the Hoyas to 87-86.

On its next possession Syracuse milked the shot clock down to five seconds, and when Georgetown's defense blinked, Coleman made it pay. "Every time I touched the ball I saw a guy coming over to double-team me," Coleman said. "So I said if he's going to double-team, it means someone else is open. I just hit the open man." And Stephen Thompson, the open man, didn't miss.

Georgetown still had two more chances to tie or win. Mutombo made one foul shot with 9 seconds left to make it 89-87, and when the miss of his second attempt went out-of-bounds off Coleman, the Hoyas had another life. However, Mourning threw up an air ball along the left baseline, and when the clock ran out the Dome turned into a circus as the fans rushed the court in celebration. "This was the kind of game that you try to carry into the tournaments," said Stephen Thompson. "It's the kind of game that should make you tougher."

Unfortunately for the Orangemen, it didn't work out that way. The next weekend they lost to UConn in the Big East Tournament title game, 78-75, then advanced only to the Sweet 16 of the NCAA Tournament where they were bounced out by Minnesota, 82-75, at the New Orleans Superdome.

Orange Slice—Billy Owens

It's not like North Carolina's Dean Smith or Villanova's Rollie Massimino really had a chance to sign Billy Owens to play for them, given the fact that Owens's older brother, Michael, was a star on the Syracuse football team and Mom and Pop Owens preferred that Billy join Michael in the land of the Carrier Dome. But then Orange basketball coach Jim Boeheim traveled into central Pennsylvania to watch Billy play in an outdoor pickup game one summer night before Billy entered his senior year at Carlisle High, and the decision was made: there was no way Boeheim was going to let this potential superstar slip through his grasp. "I don't want to sound corny," Boeheim told *Sports Illustrated* when recalling that encounter, "but to watch him play was like seeing a work of art. I walked away from there shaking my head saying to myself 'I've got to get this kid.' " Boeheim got him, and as true as Owens's jump shot was that night when he scored, by Boeheim's count, sixty-three points, Owens lived up to the billing.

Before there was Carmelo Anthony at Syracuse, there was Billy Owens, who remains one of the four or five best high school players Boeheim has ever seen. Owens led Carlisle—coached by Dave Lebo, father of one-time North Carolina star guard Jeff Lebo who was Owens's teammate—to four consecutive state championships, a fabled high school career that ended with a 113-9 record and 3,298 points. As a Carlisle freshman he was a skinny—albeit talented—shooting forward, but by the time Boeheim got wind of him on the recruiting trail, Owens was a do-everything player in the mold of his idol, Magic Johnson.

When Jim Boeheim went down to Pennsylvania to recruit Billy Owens, he remarked that he had never seen a better high school player. Owens came to Syracuse and scored 1,840 points, second only to Dave Bing among players who played three years for the Orangemen.

Like Anthony, Owens arrived at Syracuse a bit frail for the rigors of the Big East Conference, and like Anthony, by the end of his freshman season he had bulked up and become a force. He scored 13 points and grabbed 7 rebounds per game during that 1988–1989 season while sharing the court with luminaries such as Derrick Coleman, Sherman Douglas, and Stevie Thompson. As a sophomore the numbers increased to 18.2 points and 8.4 rebounds, and in his third and final year at Syracuse he averaged a double-double with 23.3 points and 11.6 rebounds per game. For comparison, in Anthony's only year at Syracuse he averaged 22.2 points and 8.7 rebounds.

Although that 1990–1991 season was marvelous from an individual standpoint, Owens's Syracuse career came to a sour end. The Orangemen—after winning their second straight Big East regular-season title—lost in the first round of the Big East Tournament to Villanova, then became the first number-two seed in history to lose to a number fifteen when Richmond took Syracuse out in the first round of the NCAA Tournament.

The three Syracuse teams Owens played on went 82-21, he was Big East player of the year in 1991, and when he left he ranked sixth all time in scoring with 1,840 points, sixth in rebounding with 910, and seventh in assists with 381.

He became the third overall pick in the 1991 draft by Sacramento, was immediately traded to Golden State, and that set a precedent that defined his NBA career. Owens never seemed to find his niche in the pro game and became a pawn in a number of trades. He switched jerseys eight times while playing for six different teams before being cut by Portland in its 2002 training camp. "There's been a lot of injuries and not living up to the goals I had," Owens said of a NBA career that saw him average 11.7 points and 6.7 rebounds.

Billy Owens

Date of birth: May 1, 1969

Hometown: Carlisle, Pennsylvania

Honors: Two-time All-American including consensus first team in 1991. . . . In 1989 was first-team freshman All-American. . . . 1991 player of the year finalist. . . . Two-time first-team All–Big East and 1991 Big East player of the year.

Achievements: One of the greatest all-around players in school history, he led SU in scoring twice, in steals twice, and in rebounds once. . . . Scored in double figures in thirty-seven straight games. . . . Was number-three overall pick in 1991 NBA draft by Sacramento.

SU career totals: 1,840 points, 910 rebounds, 381 assists, 216 steals, 97 blocked shots.

20

Easy Riter

May 31, 1993   *When Syracuse won the 1993 lacrosse na-*
Byrd Stadium   *tional championship, it was a sweet vic-*
College Park, Maryland   *tory indeed as Matt Riter's last-second*
goal enabled the Orangemen to defeat
North Carolina and avenge a season-
opening loss they had suffered to the Tar
Heels.

It was opening day of the 1993 college lacrosse season, and as Syracuse attackman Matt Riter was walking off the field in Chapel Hill, he shook hands with one of his North Carolina counterparts and passed along a message. "I told the guy who was guarding me 'I'll see you Memorial Day,' " Riter recalled.

The inference was unmistakable. North Carolina had gotten the best of the Orangemen that afternoon, 14-10, and it was clear to Riter that the Tar Heels were an awfully impressive team. But Riter had every faith that Syracuse would shake off this defeat, and if the Tar Heels did indeed reach the Division I national championship game, played annually on Memorial Day, they would be staring across the field at Riter and his fellow Orangemen. "Sure enough, we ended up getting there and we beat them," Riter said.

And how appropriate it was that Riter—unfazed by the early defeat and so confident in the ability of the Orangemen—scored the game-winning goal, one of those you-never-forget-as-long-as-you-live story-book jobs that came with eight seconds left to play and ended one of the best championship games of all time in Syracuse's favor, 13-12. "That goal was pretty special. I still hear about it today," said Riter, who was born and raised just south of Syracuse in the town of Homer and still lives there with his wife and daughter, working as a graphic designer. "I went right to the cage. I was thinking 'Oh God, don't miss it.' I made [North Carolina goalie Gary Lehrman] hesitate and shot to the weak side. I prayed it would go in."

It went in, securing Syracuse's fifth national championship in the past eleven years, but its first since Riter's freshman season of 1990 when the Orangemen were led by the indomitable Gait twins, Paul and Gary. "That was a special team because we were a bunch of country boys that jelled together," said Riter, who in 1993 scored 49 goals to earn first-team All-American honors as well as the Division I attackman of the year award. "We didn't have a lot of great players, but we had a lot of good players. It wasn't like the Paul and Gary Gait teams, but we all played together and our main focus was to win the national championship, and we did it."

Syracuse had become the preeminent lacrosse program in the 1980s when it reached its first Final Four in 1983 and won its first championship that season, edging perennial powerhouse Johns Hopkins. Four more years passed without a title as Syracuse lost twice in the finals to Hopkins before the Gaits arrived on the Hill and the Orangemen won three in a row, a feat matched only by Johns Hopkins (1978–1980) and later by Princeton (1996–1998).

In 1992 there was another championship game loss, this time in double overtime to Princeton, so the Orangemen were on the prowl again in '93, but this dog wasn't hunting early that year. The loss to North Carolina was followed two weeks later by a shocking loss to Loyola, and for the first time since 1977 Syracuse was staring at a 1-2 record.

There were many lacrosse experts who didn't think Syracuse would be able to extend its streak of consecutive Final Four appearances to eleven, but no one wearing orange was thinking like that. Syracuse found its groove, and over the next month it blew out Towson State, Brown, Hobart, Cornell, Rutgers, and Penn, then closed the regular season with solid wins over UMass and Johns Hopkins. Thanks to that eight-game winning streak Syracuse stood 9-2 and entered the NCAAs as the third seed, meaning it would have a first-round bye and then a quarterfinal home game at the Carrier Dome against Hofstra.

Hofstra was no match, losing 29-8, as Riter scored a career-high seven goals. Syracuse was on its way to the Final Four at the University of Maryland.

In the national semifinals the Orangemen avenged their championship game loss to Princeton a year earlier with a convincing 15-9 victory, and when North Carolina was just as impressive in a 16-10 romp over Johns Hopkins, Riter's prediction, made way back in early March, became reality. Hello again, Tar Heels.

In its first 15 games North Carolina had allowed an average of just 29 shots per game. Syracuse fired 25 in the first quarter alone as it dominated play. To the credit of Lehrman, the score was only 5-3 Syracuse after 15 minutes. "We didn't come out slow, they came out fast," Tar Heels defenseman Greg Paradine said. "They have a lot of great shooters."

North Carolina regrouped in the second quarter and scored five times against Syracuse goalie Chris Surran, the last by Mike Acee in a man-up situation 35 seconds before halftime to take an 8-7 lead into intermission.

Back came Syracuse as Charlie Lockwood ripped one past Lehrman 54 seconds into the second half to spur a three-goal run that produced a 10-8 lead before North Carolina drew even by the end of the third quarter on goals by John Webster and Steve Speers. After some tense moments when both goalies made big saves to preserve the tie, the Orangemen grabbed the lead when Dom Fin scored an unassisted goal, and then with 3:45 remaining Roy Colsey scored an extra-man goal off a Lockwood feed to give Syracuse a 12-10 lead.

But just when it looked like North Carolina had nothing left, Jason Wade beat Surran with 1:56 left, and 32 seconds later Donnie McNichol tied it, sending the crowd of 19,965 into a frenzy. "It was important for us not to lose our cool and to know we could put one in," said Syracuse attackman Steve Bettinger, one of five Orangemen to score two goals in this game.

Syracuse won the ensuing face-off and put heavy pressure on Lehrman over the next minute without success, and with about 25 seconds remaining North Carolina gained possession and appeared primed to have the last opportunity. However, Tar Heels coach Dave Klarmann elected not to call time-out, and it proved to be a costly decision. "I know I'll be questioned about not calling a timeout, but I thought we could settle and score," said Klarmann, who elected to let his team try to clear and possibly catch Syracuse off balance on defense. "But you can't just point to one play. This game was going to be a one-goal game no matter what."

Syracuse long-stick defenseman Ric Beardsley checked North Carolina's T. J. Shimaitis just before he reached the Orange defensive zone and jarred the ball loose. Regy Thorpe scooped the ground ball and passed to Hans Schmid near midfield. He in turn fed Lockwood, and when Tar Heel defenseman Alex Martin came after Lockwood, Riter was suddenly all alone near the restraining line. Lockwood whipped a perfect pass, and it was Riter and Lehrman, one-on-one, with the national championship hanging in the balance. "We practiced unsettled situations every day in practice," said Riter. "As soon as the ball went on the ground, I broke to the seam and Charlie got me the ball and there was no one around. I just zipped through and the goalie really didn't have a chance. My defender went up to guard [Lockwood] and didn't realize I was coming." Said Martin: "I left Riter to try and stay with the ball. I felt I had to do that. But in hindsight, I should have stayed with him."

Riter can still see himself scoring the goal today. He faked low left, shot upper right, and the net danced as Riter threw his arms up in celebration, soon to be joined by his teammates.

"I think it was good for the game today," said Syracuse coach Roy Simmons Jr. "I think people out there were applauding the lacrosse, not particularly the blue or the orange. Any time you get the Heels and Orange together, you are going to have exciting contests. We know they're explosive, and so are we." Count Yale coach Mike Waldvogel among the entertained. "This game was unbelievable," he said. "I'm out of breath from watching it."

Riter's winning goal was his tournament-leading 10th and it was the last of his 128-goal Syracuse career that, at the time of his graduation, ranked him seventh on the all-time Orange list. Riter played four seasons of pro lacrosse in the Major Indoor Lacrosse League with Rochester, scoring 28 goals and 59 points in 35 career games, and he helped the Knighthawks to the 1997 league championship.

Orange Slice—Roy Simmons Sr. and Roy Simmons Jr.

It stands as the proudest moment in the storied history of the Syracuse lacrosse program, the evening of February 8, 1992, when Roy Simmons Sr.—already a member of the National Lacrosse Hall of Fame—presented his son, Roy Jr., for induction into the sport's shrine. On that night in a hotel ballroom in Towson, Maryland, two generations of greatness stood side by side, a double-barrel dose of Syracuse lacrosse history. "It's the proudest day of my life to see him make it," Roy Sr. said that night. "It's a hell of an achievement."

The name "Simmons" is synonymous with Syracuse lacrosse the way the number 44 is synonymous with Syracuse football. It began in 1923 when Roy Sr. came to Syracuse from the University of Chicago to play quarterback for the Orangemen, then picked up a lacrosse stick, which, as legend has it, he at first thought was a crabbing net. He started fiddling around with that stick, decided to give the game a try, and within a year became an All-American defenseman who helped the 1924 and '25 teams of Laurie Cox share the United States Intercollegiate Lacrosse Association championship.

Upon graduation Roy Sr. served as an assistant football coach and as head coach of the Syracuse boxing team before taking the reins of the lacrosse program from Cox in 1931. Over the next forty years Roy Sr. produced a record of 253-130-1, a .660 winning percentage, mentoring All-Americans such as William Fuller, George Cody, Oren Lyons, Jim Ridlon, Roy Jr., and a fellow named Jim Brown. In all, 70 of Roy Sr.'s players earned 101 All-American selections and 9 are—like he and his son—enshrined in the Hall of Fame. "He is one of the finest men I've ever met in my entire life," said Brown. "When I went to Syracuse he opened his arms to me and welcomed me into a situation that was not very friendly, and that meant everything to my whole career because he was always positive, always encouraging me. Great men like Roy Simmons, they don't deal with race; they deal with people. My last year in lacrosse, I played lacrosse just because he was the coach. I wouldn't have played otherwise."

Roy Jr., who had been around Syracuse lacrosse since the late 1930s when he was the team's mascot, graduated in 1959 with a degree in sculpture, and while pursuing his love of art, he became his father's as-

Roy Simmons Sr. coached the Syracuse lacrosse team for forty years, and in the mid- to late 1950s one of his star players was his son, Roy Jr.

sistant that year. His long-range goal was to someday have Roy Sr. pass the baton, and that day came in 1970.

Over the next twenty-eight years Roy Jr. took Syracuse lacrosse to unprecedented heights. After surviving the mid-1970s when funding was nonexistent and the Orangemen suffered three consecutive losing seasons for the first time in school history, Roy Jr. began to build a powerhouse by tapping into the rich high school talent base in central New York.

With his father watching ever so proudly, Syracuse lacrosse hit the big time in 1979 when it qualified for the NCAA Tournament—started in 1971—for the first time. By 1983 the Orangemen were national champions, having defeated Johns Hopkins, and Roy Jr. was able to hand the championship plaque to his father in the celebratory locker room.

Roy Jr. went on to win 290 of the 386 games he coached at Syracuse, a winning percentage of .751. During his last eleven years his record was an incredible 138-22, a winning percentage of .862, and he won five of his six national championships in that stretch. Seventy of his players earned a combined 138 All-American selections, with Brad Kotz, Gary Gait, and Casey Powell winning a total of five national player of the year awards. Roy Jr. led the Orangemen to the Final Four in each of his last sixteen years.

Despite all the success, to a man, every Syracuse athlete who ever played for Roy Jr. speaks first of the person he is rather than the great coach that he was. "I think that everybody's life is a little bit different that's been able to play for Coach Simmons," said Ryan Powell. "He just has an unbelievable impact on people." John Desko, a former player under Roy Jr. who later became his top assistant and then took over as head coach when Roy Jr. retired after the 1998 season, said, "When he talks to his team, they listen. A lot of people compare it to an E. F. Hutton commercial: when Roy talks you listen. You learned a lot more about life than just lacrosse from Roy Simmons, Jr." And the greatest player Simmons ever coached, Gary Gait, also hammers home the point that Simmons helped redefine how the game is played by the way he allowed Gary and Paul Gait to flourish during their years at Syracuse: "Coach Simmons was the catalyst for developing a new style of play," Gary said. "He allowed Paul, myself and Tom Marechek the freedom to be creative and change the style of college lacrosse. To have that vision is pretty unique. A lot of coaches would not allow that and I think he looked at us as if we were artists with lacrosse sticks."

Roy Simmons Sr.

Date of birth: September 27, 1901

Hometown: Philadelphia, Pennsylvania

Honors: Member of the National Lacrosse Hall of Fame, the Greater Syracuse Sports Hall of Fame, and the Upstate New York Chapter of the Lacrosse Foundation Hall of Fame. . . . Earned All-American recognition as a player in 1924.

Achievements: Captain of SU's 1924 and '25 national championship lacrosse teams. . . . Played quarterback for the football team and boxed during his undergrad days. . . . Was head lacrosse coach for forty years. . . . Was SU boxing coach for thirty-one years. . . . Was assistant football coach. . . . His teams won fourteen eastern championships.

SU career totals: Record of 253-130-1 as head lacrosse coach from 1931 to 1970.

Roy Simmons Jr.

Date of birth: August 6, 1935

Hometown: Syracuse, New York

Honors: Member of the National Lacrosse Hall of Fame, the Greater Syracuse Sports Hall of Fame, and the Upstate New York Chapter of the Lacrosse Foundation Hall of Fame. . . . Selected as a Syracuse Letterman of Distinction in 1984. . . . NCAA coach of the year in 1980. . . . Two-time All-American as a player in 1957 and '58.

Achievements: One of only two coaches to win six national championships, and one of only three coaches to win three straight titles. . . . His thirty-four NCAA tournament victories are a record, as are his nineteen tournament appearances and his sixteen straight Final Four appearances.

SU career totals: 290-96-0 as head lacrosse coach from 1971 to 1998.

21

Kentucky Blues

April 1, 1996
Continental Airlines Arena
East Rutherford, New Jersey

An ESPN.com opinion piece in 2003 provided a list of what the authors believed were the ten greatest college basketball teams of all-time, and they ranked Rick Pitino's 1996 Kentucky squad number two behind only the Lew Alcindor–John Wooden 1968 UCLA team. Syracuse was a huge underdog the night it faced Kentucky for the 1996 national championship, and only John Wallace's determination and leadership enabled the Orangemen to stay close.

Until the end, the very bitter end, John Wallace believed that Syracuse was going to win the 1996 national championship. As far back as the summer of 1995, when Wallace bucked conventional wisdom and announced his intention to return to Syracuse for his senior year rather than chase the riches of the NBA, Wallace believed he could deliver to coach Jim Boeheim that elusive first NCAA title.

Into October when practice began at Manley Field House, Wallace believed in the Orange. Never mind that Syracuse had bowed out the previous March in the second round of the NCAA Tournament and had bid farewell to the school's all-time leading scorer, Lawrence Moten. Never mind that the Orangemen were ranked an unflattering thirty-third in the preseason Associated Press poll and no one considered them a threat to reach the championship game of the Big East Tournament,

166

John Wallace seriously considered jumping to the NBA following his junior season, but he stuck around to play as a senior, and he led the Orangemen to the national championship game where they lost to Kentucky.

let alone the ultimate game, the game that defines college basketball careers.

Wallace's belief only strengthened when the snow began to fall in central New York and the Orangemen reeled off eleven straight victories to start the season, most notably a hugely impressive road conquest of then number three Arizona that was just the Wildcats' second non-conference home loss in eight years. And then, even when things began to unravel as Syracuse lost six of its next nine, and eventually was out-classed 85-67 by UConn in the semifinals of the Big East Tournament, Wallace's belief never wavered.

And now, as Wallace was walking off the floor at Continental Airlines Arena after having fouled out, his Orangemen down five points to Kentucky with just 66 seconds remaining in the final game of the season, the final game of his illustrious career, Wallace still believed. "Win it for us," he said to teammate Otis Hill. "You can win it."

Of course, they did not win. In truth, they could not win. Probably not even with Wallace still on the court, certainly not with him sitting helplessly on the bench. Wallace had dared to believe, and thanks largely to his skill and his will Syracuse had enjoyed a glorious run to the grandest stage in college basketball. But on this night there would be no national championship for Wallace, Boeheim, and the rest of the Orangemen. "John Wallace stepped up as big as anyone has ever done for us," Boeheim said following his second defeat in an NCAA title game, a disappointing 76-67 loss to Rick Pitino's supremely talented Wildcats. Boeheim was speaking particularly about this game, but he might as well have been referencing the entire 1995–1996 season.

When Boeheim took the Orangemen to the 1987 championship game where it lost to Indiana, he guided a marvelously talented team that featured future NBA players Derrick Coleman, Rony Seikaly, and Sherman Douglas, plus a supporting cast that included Stephen Thompson, Greg Monroe, Howard Triche, and Derek Brower.

The 1995–1996 team? Wallace, one of the finest players to ever pull on an Orange jersey, was truly a star as he finished his career as Syracuse's number-three all-time scorer and rebounder. But all around him were modestly talented players such as Hill, Todd Burgan, Lazarus Sims, Jason Cipolla, and sixth man Marius Janulis.

They had hearts so big you could see them beating in their chests, and they had enough grit to cover the roof of the Carrier Dome. Yet although those attributes, combined with Wallace's brilliance, helped Syracuse reach the swamps of New Jersey on this April Fool's night, they weren't enough to get them past a Kentucky team that would ultimately produce five first-round NBA draft picks in Antoine Walker, Tony Delk, Walter McCarty, Derek Anderson, and Ron Mercer and a second-rounder in Mark Pope. "I was just thinking about all the hard work in the preseason, all the weightlifting, all the running to get to this point," Burgan said as he watched Kentucky celebrate. "We didn't get over the hump and win the national championship, but I was proud. You have a lot of mixed emotions, but you have to be very, very proud because there were a lot of teams that were home just wishing they could be in this position." And there was so much to be proud of as this Syracuse team produced one of the most surprising and rewarding years in Boeheim's highly successful tenure.

The run through the NCAA Tournament took root in Albuquerque, New Mexico, where Syracuse began play as the number-four seed in the West Regional. The Orangemen opened with an 88-55 rout of over-matched Montana State, a game so one-sided that even a certain Philadelphia Eagles star quarterback named Donovan McNabb, then a reserve guard for Boeheim, saw three minutes of playing time, scoring one basket. When the Orangemen slipped past Drexel 69-58, it was on to Denver for the Sweet 16.

There, on a fabulous Friday night a mile above sea level, Cipolla knocked down a twelve-foot leaner at the buzzer to force overtime, and then Wallace drained a twenty-one-foot three-pointer with 2.8 seconds left in the extra period to defeat Georgia, 83-81, in one of the most memorable games in Syracuse history.

Two days later, with a spot in the Final Four up for grabs, the fourth-seeded Orangemen met up with second-seeded Kansas, a Roy Williams club that would send Paul Pierce, Raef Lafrentz, Scot Pollard, and Jacque Vaughn to the NBA. But that star-studded Jayhawk lineup shot just four-for-twenty-five from three-point land against the Syracuse zone, and with Wallace and Hill scoring fifteen points apiece, Syracuse won the West with a 60-57 victory. "Who picked us to make the Final Four," said Wallace, who returned to Syracuse for that sole purpose, and made it there. "Probably nobody. But we believed and now we're going to New Jersey. I couldn't have written a better script, in terms of the way things finally worked out for me. It's a dream come true. But at the same time, it's not enough just to go to the Final Four. Now we want to win the whole thing."

Next up was another unlikely Final Four participant, Mississippi State, a team that had blown through UConn and Cincinnati on its way up the Jersey Turnpike. The Bulldogs were formidable, and while they outrebounded the Orangemen 40-21, they lost where it counted most, on the scoreboard, 77-69.

When Kentucky punched its ticket a couple hours later by beating UMass 81-74, the final was set, and naturally the Orangemen were prohibitive underdogs. "It's been that way from the start," said Wallace.

But this was different. This was Kentucky with all those great players, a team that had won thirty-three of thirty-five games to date thanks to frenetic offense and in-your-face, baseline-to-baseline pressure defense. The point spread was fourteen, the largest since the 1972 final that pitted John Wooden's dynastic UCLA team against Florida State. No one expected it to be close, but Wallace was undeterred. "We don't care what the spread is or who thinks we're not going to win," he said, defiant as ever. "As long as we think we're going to win, that's all that matters."

Well, not quite. With Delk hammering home six three-pointers on his way to a championship game record-tying seven, Kentucky surged to a 42-33 halftime lead. Syracuse fought back to 48-46, but the Wildcats answered with an 11-0 run that extended the margin to 59-46 with 11:12 remaining, the spurt capped by a rare four-point play as Delk hit his last three-pointer and made a free throw after Burgan fouled him.

Maybe those guys in Vegas knew something Wallace and the Orangemen didn't. Then again, maybe not. Burgan scored a fast-break basket, and then Sims—who had broken his wrist in the first half but played the second half with it heavily bandaged—drove and dished off to Wallace for a dunk. Burgan's three-pointer with 8:56 to go pulled the Orangemen to 62-55, and Wallace turned another jam on a pretty move into a three-point play.

Four minutes later, thanks to a Wallace layup and a pair of free throws, Syracuse had cut its deficit to 64-62, the arena was abuzz, Billy Packer was praising the gutty Orangemen, the Wildcats were askew, and Wallace was woofing the way he always woofed. "We put ourselves in position to win the basketball game," Boeheim said. "And then Kentucky made some great plays."

The first came when McCarty soared above the rim to tip in a missed three-pointer by Delk, and then Anderson rattled home a three-pointer to make it 69-62, and just like that the Wildcats were back in control.

"Every time we got within two or four points," Sims said, "they hit a three or got an offensive rebound. And that set us back for the simple fact we were playing so hard to get in that position."

There was one last gasp for Syracuse, and it ended with a gasp. Trailing 72-67 with possession and just over a minute left on the clock, Sims drove into the lane and tried to dish off to Wallace. The forced pass was deflected by Pope, and as Pope tried to corral the loose ball Wallace pushed him. The sellout crowd was screaming, but everyone could hear loudly and clearly the shrill whistle of referee John Clougherty, and when Clougherty raised one arm and pointed at Wallace with the other, he pulled the plug on Syracuse's comeback effort. The foul on Wallace ended his career, and the Orange's hopes. "We needed to make that play right there," said Boeheim. "That was the play. That was the game play."

With Wallace unable to watch, a towel draped over his head, Pope made the foul shots, and Kentucky—its storied program embarrassingly disgraced and in shambles before Pitino rescued it—was the undisputed king of the college hardwood again. "There were a couple of questionable calls," said Wallace, who finished with a game-high 29 points and 10 rebounds. "It was such a bad feeling to foul out and leave your team hanging like that. At no point during the game did I feel like we were going to lose. We played very good and we should have won the game." Still believing, even a half hour after the Wildcats had snipped the nets off the rims.

But that was Wallace. That was this Syracuse team. So much heart, but not quite enough skill to pull off what would have been one of the all-time NCAA shockers. "I have never tried to play up the underdog role with this team," said Boeheim. "They go into each game thinking they should win. They still think they should have won tonight. That's the kind of attitude you want your team to have. I told the players in the locker room that too much is made that you lost the game. They didn't lose anything to me. If sports is supposed to be about good things, then this team is about good things. They gave everything they had. I think they're champions."

The Orangemen finally attained that elusive national championship in 2003 when Carmelo Anthony led them to an 81-79 NCAA title-game victory over Kansas. Kentucky played in the next two championship games, losing to Ari-

zona in 1997 and beating Utah in 1998. Wallace became a first-round pick of the New York Knicks in 1996, number eighteen overall, but he never really made a major impact. He later played for Toronto, the Knicks again, Detroit, and Phoenix and averaged eight points and three rebounds per game in the NBA. He has been playing overseas since 2002.

Orange Slice—Lazarus Sims

It was just like old times for Lazarus Sims in November 2003 when he took the floor at the Carrier Dome to a huge ovation from the 20,000-plus on hand, and then left the floor a couple hours later with another victory in his hip pocket, a common occurrence during his playing days at Syracuse. One difference: Sims was not playing for the Orangemen, his hometown team that he had helped lead to the 1996 NCAA national championship game. On that special night at the Dome Sims was back in the city of his birth wearing the visitors' uniform, that of basketball's most beloved ensemble, the Harlem Globetrotters.

During their 2003 College Fall Tour the Globetrotters played serious basketball as a way to prepare for the upcoming season of their patented, world-famous brand of show-time basketball. The Globetrotters played eight games against top-notch Division I college teams, and when they visited Syracuse they hung an 83-70 defeat on the defending national champion Orangemen.

Sims—a Henninger High grad who still lives in Syracuse in the off-season and does community work at the Southwest Community Center, Kirk Park, the Shonnard Street Boys, and Girls Club and numerous other youth facilities in the city—had 9 points, 4 rebounds, and 9 assists. Those statistics mirrored the ones he used to accumulate while playing for the Orangemen. Nothing flashy, nothing spectacular. Just solid, lunch-bucket work that every team needs to succeed.

It took five years for Sims to finally break into Jim Boeheim's starting lineup, and his perseverance paid off when, in 1995–1996, his leadership and playmaking at the point was one of the keys to Syracuse's run to the title game where it lost to Kentucky. "I still haven't watched a tape of that game; it's too painful," said Sims, who averaged 6.4 points and 7.4 assists per game that season while logging only fifteen fewer minutes on the court than his good friend and the star of the team, John Wallace. "A lot of people thought we were a fluke. But we all believed we could beat Kentucky."

After graduating, Sims tried to continue his career, but when the NBA showed no interest, he hit the minor league trail and played in the CBA, the IBA, and even spent some time playing professionally in Poland and Venezuela. In 2001 he earned a tryout with the NBA's Memphis Grizzlies but was cut early in the preseason. "That was pretty much it for me as far as the NBA was concerned," Sims said. "I was closing in on 30. It was time to move on."

He went back to the CBA, then tried out for the Globetrotters in 2002, but didn't make the final cut. However, he stayed in touch with team owner Mannie Jackson, made the team in 2003, and is still barnstorming with the Globies today. "This has been one of those once-in-a-lifetime opportunities for me," he said. "The Globetrotters are probably the most famous basketball team in the world and I'm getting a chance to be a part of history. I saw them as a kid and they put on a great show. And, now, I'm a part of that show. It's special."

"He isn't the best ball handler or the best passer or the best shooter on our team, but he does everything well and he has the kind of positive personality and character we are looking for," said Jackson. "He is just a great ambassador for the game and for his school. In that regard, he reminds me a lot of another classy player from Syracuse—Dave Bing."

Lazarus Sims

Date of birth: March 28, 1972

Hometown: Syracuse, New York

Honors: Ranked number one in Big East in assists in 1995–1996, number two in the nation.

Achievements: His 281 assists as a senior were the fourth-best single-season total in school history, second most by a senior. . . . Failed to make it in the NBA, played minor league pro basketball, and now plays for the world-famous Harlem Globetrotters.

SU career totals: 385 points, 432 assists, 222 rebounds.

22

McNabb's Prayer
Is Answered

November 15, 1998   *In a career that was marked by brilliance*
Carrier Dome   *and record-breaking performances, Dono-*
Syracuse, New York   *van McNabb's finest hour—or should we*
say second—came when he threw a last-
play prayer into the end zone that resulted
in a miraculous touchdown and a victory
over Virginia Tech.

I t was nearly a full year later, but no amount of time was going to ease the pain and suffering of Virginia Tech linebacker Michael Hawkes. "I'll never forget it . . . it will always be in my mind," Hawkes said in October 1999 as he and the Hokies were preparing to host Big East rival Syracuse, the smell of blood and revenge hanging heavily in the Blacksburg, Virginia, air.

Who could blame Hawkes? How could he forget what had happened one year earlier when Virginia Tech lost, 28-26, to Syracuse on a miracle play that will live in infamy in the history of both schools? Quite simply, you don't forget the worst moment of your athletic career. Not one year later. Not ever.

The Hokies seemingly had a victory at Syracuse's Carrier Dome wrapped up, a victory that would keep alive their chances of winning the Big East title and advancing to a multimillion-dollar BCS bowl game. They led 26-22, and though the Orangemen were positioned at

174

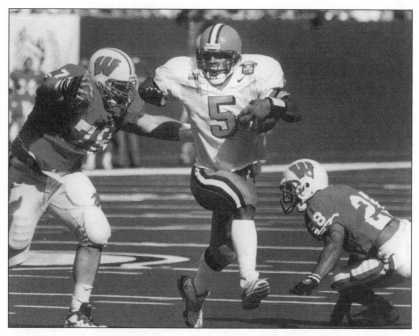

During a marvelous career that saw him voted as the Big East offensive player of the decade for the 1990s, Donovan McNabb was a dual threat who could hurt teams with his running as well as his passing. He holds the all-time Big East record for total offense with 9,950 yards.

the Tech 13, there was time for just one more play, and the confident Hokie defense—fifth best in the nation at the time—liked its chances.

Of course, the Hokies failed to take into account the wondrous talent of SU quarterback Donovan McNabb. Before they knew it McNabb was lobbing a pass into the end zone, a prayer that was answered when un- heralded tight end Stephen Brominski plucked the ball out of the air just before Hawkes could get over to knock it away, touching off a riotous celebration that made your average Syracuse-Georgetown basketball crowd sound like a book-of-the-month-club meeting. Tech punter Jimmy Kibble, who watched in horror from the numbed Virginia Tech sideline as Brominski made the catch, summed up the feelings of Hokies past, present, and future when he said, "Just to see him catch it, I dropped to my knees. It was a heart-wrenching, gut-wrenching feeling, and it's not something I'll ever forget."

It was a jaw-dropping finish, the likes of which hadn't been seen at the Dome since the magical 1987 season when Michael Owens scored on a two-point conversion in the final seconds to beat West Virginia and preserve a perfect 11-0 regular season. "That was the greatest game I've ever been a part of," Orange offensive lineman Scott Kiernan said. It was the greatest game any Orangeman had been involved in. "Don was great, great, great," Syracuse coach Paul Pasqualoni said of his star quarterback. "It was a tremendous game."

It was a game that Syracuse had dominated, but thanks to a quartet of superb Virginia Tech plays, it was a game Syracuse was losing as the clock raced toward zero. But the X factor was McNabb, and he led a breathtaking march down the field in the final seconds to pull out the victory. "We have a lot of heart and a lot of courage," said McNabb, who was 15 of 32 for 232 yards and 2 touchdowns. "I wasn't going to be down. I wasn't going to let my team down. I'm the leader, and I've got to get us in the end zone."

Here's how he did it. After taking an early 3-0 lead, the Orangemen collapsed under the weight of a 21-point Virginia Tech barrage fueled by big plays. The first came when Jarrett Ferguson broke a 76-yard touchdown run—producing exactly half of the Hokies' offensive yardage for the entire game.

Anthony Midget then blocked a punt by Syracuse's Donald Dinkins that Ricky Hall recovered in the SU end zone to put the Hokies ahead 14-3 midway through the second period. Next came a fumble by Maurice Jackson that was forced by Virginia Tech safety Keion Carpenter. The ball popped into the air where Tech cornerback Loren Johnson hauled it in and raced 78 yards for a TD.

The Dome fell silent, and even with McNabb at the controls, rallying from an eighteen-point deficit against the sixteenth-ranked Hokies seemed nearly impossible. However, the Orangemen never bowed, because they knew they had McNabb. "Donovan McNabb had the courage of a lion," Pasqualoni said moments after his one hundredth career victory. "The plays he made were just a tremendous demonstration of courage by a great leader."

Nate Trout began Syracuse's comeback with a field goal on the last play of the half to make it 21-6, and then the Orangemen tacked on ten more points in the third quarter as McNabb tossed a 1-yard TD pass to

Brominski and Trout kicked his third field goal, a 30-yarder, to pull Syracuse to 21-16.

Early in the fourth quarter a bizarre sequence saw Syracuse take the lead, then lose it, in a matter of seconds. Rob Konrad plunged into the end zone to put the Orangemen ahead 22-21, but McNabb's two-point conversion pass was intercepted by Tech's ever present Johnson. Johnson sped downfield, and when McNabb caught him at the SU 10, he fumbled the ball into the end zone and teammate Jamel Smith fell on it for a defensive two-pointer, putting the Hokies ahead 23-22.

When Shayne Graham made a 49-yard field goal with 4:42 left to play it looked like Virginia Tech was in good shape. But this is when Mc-Nabb trotted onto the field and began a 14-play, 83-yard march to pay dirt, and he used every last second of that 4:42.

Tech had Syracuse in trouble when it forced a fourth-and-7 at the Orange 44, but McNabb scrambled for a brilliant 41-yard run to the Hokies' 15 to keep the drive alive and send the Dome into a frenzy. Two plays later McNabb hit Jackson for a 14-yard gain to the 1, and with 51 seconds to go Syracuse was on the cusp of victory.

However, the proud Hokies revolted as they stuffed Konrad for no gain. After a roughing-the-passer penalty moved the ball to within two feet of the goal line, Tech's superb pass-rushing end Corey Moore sacked McNabb for a 12-yard loss. With no time-outs, McNabb regained his composure, got his team to the line, and spiked the ball to stop the clock with five ticks remaining.

On the last play of the night, McNabb wanted to pass to Kevin Johnson, but he was blanketed by a pair of Hokies. McNabb thought about running, but Tech was looking for that and they closed off his lanes. All he could do was float one into the end zone and hope the six-foot-five Brominski was up to being the hero. He was. "I told him that if he needed to come back to me, I'd be in the end zone," Brominski said. "I was aware that [Hawkes] was there, but I just had to go up and catch it." Said McNabb, "I just threw it for [Brominski's] helmet. I was hoping I had put enough on it so that [Hawkes] wouldn't knock it down. I knew Steve would catch it."

Syracuse ran 50 more offensive plays than Tech, outgained the Hokies 420-152, and had a 23-6 advantage in first downs. Still, it took a Herculean effort by the greatest quarterback in Big East Conference history to deliver the victory for Syracuse. "We had it in our hands and let it slip away," said free safety Pierson Prioleau. "You can never underestimate Donovan McNabb and Syracuse. We hounded him, in fact we probably got to him more times than anybody has before. He even threw up on the field a couple times. I credit him for fighting hard and leading his team in a big game."

Oh, did Hawkes and the Hokies get their revenge on Syracuse the following year as the Hokies laid an incredible 62-0 licking on Syracuse. In the four years that followed, Virginia Tech's program became one of the elite in the country while Syracuse began to slip from national prominence. However, although the Hokies were never ranked lower than eighth in the polls and Syracuse was unranked in each game, the Orangemen managed to split the next four, winning at Blacksburg, 22-14, in 2001 and then 50-42 in triple overtime at the Dome in 2002. Virginia Tech won the 2003 game, 51-7, and the series came to an end—for now—when the Hokies left the Big East to join the ACC in 2004.

Orange Slice—Donovan McNabb

Thick skin is a prerequisite to playing professional sports in Philadelphia, but Donovan McNabb didn't even have a chance to develop a hardened exterior. On the April 1999 afternoon when the Eagles used the number-two overall pick in the first round of the NFL draft on the Syracuse superstar instead of Texas running back Ricky Williams, a group of Philly fans at Madison Square Garden booed the selection.

Do you wonder what those same fans are thinking now that Mc-Nabb has led the Eagles to five straight playoff appearances, four consecutive NFC Championship Games, and, at long last, Philadelphia's first Super Bowl since the 1980 season? "Ricky Williams is a tremendous player," Eagles coach Andy Reid said the day he picked McNabb. "I'm not taking anything away from Ricky. On Sundays, the fans will know what we've got here."

McNabb's first Super Bowl appearance did not go well. He threw for 357 yards, the fourth-highest total in Super Bowl history, and he also had three touchdown passes. However, his three interceptions proved

Following his final game at the Carrier Dome, a resounding rout
of rival Miami, Donovan McNabb salutes the fans who in turn
sent him off to NFL stardom with a standing ovation.

enormously costly and were a key reason for Philadelphia's 24-21 loss to
New England in February 2005 at Jacksonville.

Still, Reid was right. Even those hard-to-please Eagles fans know
what they have, and what they have is one of the finest quarterbacks in

the game today, a five-time Pro Bowler who in 2004 set an Eagles record with 3,875 passing yards and became the first quarterback in NFL history to throw for at least thirty touchdowns (thirty-one) while throwing fewer than ten interceptions (eight).

McNabb was recruited by Paul Pasqualoni out of Chicago and became undoubtedly the best player who ever played under the former Syracuse coach. The sometimes hard-to-please Syracuse fans knew exactly what they had, and following McNabb's last game at the Dome, the unforgettable 66-13 rout of Miami, they let him know it. "I don't know if the fans could have cheered any harder or any louder for any guy," said Pasqualoni after he removed his star early in the fourth quarter so that the Dome denizens could salute him. "He's meant everything. He's a great football player. He's a great kid. He has done so much for his team."

With McNabb at quarterback the Orange won thirty-five of forty-nine games and three straight Big East championships, and he set eight school records, including most yards of total offense with 9,950, which still stands as the Big East record.

McNabb was even a part-time basketball player, and he once scored ten points to help the Orange defeat Georgetown in a 1997 game. Syracuse assistant basketball coach Bernie Fine said that if McNabb had concentrated solely on basketball, he probably wouldn't have been a starter, "but he would have been a consistently solid performer off the bench. But football obviously was his best sport. I think you can say he made the right decision."

And Eagles fans, despite their early reluctance, have certainly realized that Reid made the right decision, too.

Donovan McNabb

Date of birth: November 25, 1976

Hometown: Chicago, Illinois

Honors: Three-time Big East player of the year. . . . Big East offensive player of the decade (1990s). . . . Was Big East player of the week ten times. . . . All–Big East player four times. . . . Member SU All-Century Team. . . . Youngest person ever elected to the Board of Trustees at Syracuse University.

Achievements: Number-two overall pick in 1999 NFL draft by Eagles. . . . All-time Big East leader in total offense. . . . His 77 TD passes are SU record as is his 155.1 career passing-efficiency mark. . . . He ranks second all time in career completions, attempts, and passing yards behind only Marvin Graves.

SU career totals: 548 completions, 938 attempts, 8,389 passing yards, 77 TD passes, 9,950 total offensive yards, responsible for 96 TDs.

23

Exorcising Some Ghosts

April 7, 2003
Louisiana Superdome
New Orleans, Louisiana

After three unsuccessful journeys to the Final Four, the Orangemen at long last danced gleefully on college basketball's grandest stage when they defeated Kansas to win their first national championship, appropriately enough in the same venue where sixteen years earlier Jim Boeheim had endured his most bitter defeat.

Upon entering the Louisiana Superdome for practice before the start of the 2003 NCAA Final Four, Jim Boeheim couldn't help but steal a glance at the spot where Keith Smart had broken his heart sixteen years earlier. A shiver sprinted up the Syracuse University basketball coach's spine as he replayed in his mind that painful, drifting corner shot with four seconds remaining so many tournaments ago. If only the Indiana guard's jumper had found iron rather than the center of the cylinder that dramatic night in the NCAA Championship game, Boeheim would have been spared sixteen years of annoying "Why can't you win the big one?" questions. And Syracuse fans would have been spared the replays, shown ad nauseam each March, of the shot that denied them the national championship they long coveted.

As Boeheim watched his team warm up not far from where his Nightmare on Bourbon Street had occurred, he wondered if, maybe, just maybe, this might be the year the Orangemen finally exorcised the ghost of Keith Smart. What better place to do it, he thought to himself, than here.

Jim Boeheim had watched in person as Bob Knight and Rick Pitino cut down the nets after beating the Orangemen in national championship games. But in 2003, Boeheim finally earned the opportunity to climb the ladder and clip off a piece of history.

The so-called college basketball experts had low expectations for the 'Cuse heading into the season. In its preview issue, *Sports Illustrated* ranked the Orangemen fifty-third, and the Associated Press voters kept them off their top-twenty-five ballots.

Few questioned this SU team would be more talented than the 2001–2002 edition, which lost eight of its final twelve regular-season games and wound up in the less prestigious National Invitational Tournament. A great recruiting class would surely pump new life into the program. It would be led by freshman forward Carmelo Anthony, whose incandescent smile and well-rounded game reminded many of Hall of Famer Magic Johnson. Fellow freshman Gerry McNamara, a scrappy, sweet-shooting guard, had been recruited by the likes of three-time national champion Duke. And the team's other stellar recruit, Billy Edelin, had been the point guard for the nation's top-ranked high school team while playing for Oak Hill Academy in Virginia.

Despite the influx of young talent, no pundit believed a team that started two freshmen and two sophomores could make the quantum leap from missing the NCAAs one year to winning it all the next. But someone apparently forgot to tell Anthony, McNamara, and Edelin to act their age on the court. At the end of Syracuse's first practice that season, the young but supremely confident players huddled up at center court in Manley Field House and chanted in unison, "Final Four." Talk about a good omen.

Though they lost their opener to Memphis at Madison Square Garden, there were encouraging signs as Anthony established a school record for freshmen with 27 points and McNamara chipped in with 14. The Orangemen then reeled off eleven consecutive victories, including a 76-69 win over Missouri, then ranked eleventh in the nation.

The 'Cuse continued to open eyes by storming back from double-digit deficits to defeat second-ranked Pittsburgh and ninth-ranked Notre Dame in the Carrier Dome. But it wasn't until the Orangemen came away with victories at three of the toughest venues in college basketball—Michigan State, Notre Dame, and Georgetown—that outsiders began to take them seriously. "I think those wins on the road convinced people that this team might just be capable of doing something extraordinary," Boeheim said. "Maybe these kids really were too young to realize that you aren't supposed to win three games in places like that or to come back from so many big deficits. There probably were five or six games that season we had no business winning because we had dug ourselves too big a hole. But somehow, some way, they found a way to come back." Fifteen times the Orangemen staged second-half comebacks. No wonder some scribes started referring to them as Cardiac 'Cuse.

Sparked by Anthony (22.2 points and 10 rebounds per game), McNamara (13.3 points and nearly 5 assists per game), and sophomore forward Hakim Warrick (14.8 and 8.5 rebounds per game), the Orangemen finished the regular season 23-4 and easily earned an NCAA Tournament bid. SU wound up losing by 13 points to Connecticut in the Big East Tournament semifinals, but the defeat had no effect on its postseason momentum.

Syracuse staved off Manhattan in its NCAA opener, then bounced back from an 18-point deficit to defeat Oklahoma State in Boston. From there the Orangemen moved to the East Regional finals in Albany, where they enjoyed a home-away-from-home-court advantage at the Pepsi Center. They squeaked by Auburn, 79-78, in the regional opener, then annihilated Oklahoma, 63-47, to earn a trip to the Final Four in New Orleans. "I had a tremendous experience for five days, 39 minutes and 56 seconds there," Boeheim said when asked how it felt to be going back to the Bayou. "I'm gonna try to get that other four seconds in this time." Though underdogs, Syracuse easily handled Texas in the national semifinal, 95-84, setting the stage for its third trip to the championship game.

The title match pitted two coaches—Boeheim and Roy Williams of Kansas—who had come away empty in this game before. In fact, it was noted quite often by commentators before the game that Boeheim was the coach with the most tournament victories without a championship.

The Jayhawks entered as favorites, but McNamara proved too much for them to handle from the start. G-Mac clearly was in a shooter's zone that first half, pumping in a title-game record six threes as the Orangemen sped to an incredible 18-point lead. Although Kansas managed to pare the deficit to 53-42 by intermission, SU appeared in complete control, and that King Kong was teetering on Boeheim's back, ready to tumble.

But, as fate would have it, the Jayhawks staged a furious comeback in the second half that saw them slice the deficit to just 3 points as the clock wound down. SU had a chance to salt it away from the free-throw line, but just as had happened during the '87 title game, the Orangemen failed to capitalize. Kansas had an opportunity to tie the game on its last possession and send it into overtime. SU coaches, players, and fans couldn't believe what was unfolding. They were experiencing a bad case of déjà blue. Boeheim admitted:

I was having flashbacks to '87 during the final seconds. I'm not thinking good thoughts when Kansas is bringing the ball down the court. We had just missed a few free throws—just like '87—and I look to the corner, and I saw [Michael] Lee open, just like Smart was. It actually worked out for us because we had our centers out and we had put Hakim in at center. We didn't do it for defensive reasons, but rather because I wanted to have our best ballhandlers and shooters on the floor. If we had our centers in, it's doubtful one of them would have come out to contest Lee. But

Hakim was thinking like a forward, so he went out there. It was an incredible play on his part. I still don't know how he got to that ball.

But he did, and he wound up rejecting the shot and the notion that
history was about to repeat itself. "Same building, same part of the
court, similar situation," Boeheim said. "If that had gone in . . ." He
paused for a second, then finished his sentence, saying, "They probably
wouldn't have let me back into town." Instead, he became the toast of
the town.

The Jayhawks inbounded the ball after Warrick's block and were
way off with their final shot. The buzzer sounded on SU's 81-78 victory,
and the Orangemen piled on top of one another at center court. It had
truly been a total team effort.

McNamara, who finished with 18 points, had set the tone with his
dead-on marksmanship. Anthony, despite a back so painful he could
barely reach down to tie his shoes, earned most outstanding player honors with 20 points, 10 rebounds, and 7 assists. Warrick had just 6 points
and 2 rebounds, but his block was a game saver. And Edelin and Josh
Pace came off the bench to combine for 20 points, 10 rebounds, 4 assists,
and 6 steals. "Every guy contributed, even the walk-ons who pushed us
in practice," said senior guard Kueth Duany, who added 11 points. "The
bottom line is that we were a complete team."

From Marshall Street to Bourbon Street, SU supporters celebrated
wildly. Even Boeheim, the man *Sports Illustrated* labeled "coaching's favorite curmudgeon," let his thinning hair down. Surrounded by family
and players past and present on the Superdome court, Boeheim shed a
tear as he peered at the scoreboard to make sure this wasn't a dream.

Later, he and his wife, Juli, led a procession of hundreds of adoring
Syracuse fans, Pied Piper–style, through New Orleans's French Quarter.
Before calling it a night in the wee hours of that Tuesday morning, a fan
presented Juli with an orange velour cowboy hat. Her husband would
wear it at several functions honoring the team in Syracuse, showing a
humorous side that he hadn't always made public.

The nation witnessed Boeheim's self-deprecating personality when
he traded barbs with David Letterman on national television and felt his
pride when he and Anthony rang the opening bell at the New York
Stock Exchange. (It should be noted that the luck of the Orange was felt
on Wall Street that day as the Dow climbed 147 points.)

Just five days after knocking off the Jayhawks, more than 25,000 fans congregated in the Carrier Dome to say thanks amid an atmosphere that resembled a high-energy rock concert. "The most enjoyable part about it was the impact it has had on our fans and our alumni," Boeheim said. "I can't tell you the number of times I've been out speaking when someone will come up to me and say, 'Thanks, coach, I don't have to hear about that damn Keith Smart any more.' "

With Anthony off making millions in the NBA in 2003–2004, the Orange made a gallant effort to defend their title, but fell short. With McNamara and Warrick stepping into starring roles, Syracuse went 20-6 in the regular season, including 13-3 in the Big East. Following a shocking loss to Boston College in the Big East Tournament, the Orangemen survived the first two rounds of the NCAA Tournament before bowing to Alabama, 80-71, in the Sweet 16 at Phoenix. They finished with a record of 23-8.

Orange Slice—Carmelo Anthony

Carmelo Anthony was a member of the Syracuse University basketball team for just one season before taking his dazzling act to the NBA. As it turned out, one season was enough time for him to make an impression that will last for as long as the Orange play hoops.

Though just an eighteen-year-old freshman during the 2002–2003 season, Anthony displayed the basketball skills of a seasoned pro, averaging 22 points and 10 rebounds as the Orangemen won their first NCAA basketball championship. Many regard it as the best freshman season in the history of college basketball.

At six-foot-eight, 225 pounds, Anthony was strong enough to mix it up with the big guys underneath, but it was his all-around game that made him special. He was quick for his size and had the ball-handling skills of a guard. He also possessed an accurate outside shot. "I really think there were times that season when he was unstoppable," said Jim Boeheim, who called Anthony the most gifted player he has coached. "If you didn't go out and cover him, he'd hit the 3, and if you did go out and cover him, he'd dribble by you as if you were just standing still."

Interestingly, the player known simply as Melo almost jumped directly from high school to the NBA. It was only after his mother urged him to give college a shot that he wound up at Syracuse. Both player and

Carmelo Anthony played only year on the Hill, but what a year it was. The silky-smooth forward averaged 22.2 points and 10 rebounds in leading the Orangemen to their only college basketball national championship.

program benefited. Sporting a high-wattage smile reminiscent of basketball legend Magic Johnson, Anthony played with a little boy's joy
that endeared him to the Orange faithful. "We knew he'd be a special
player," Boeheim said. "After the first few practices we weren't talking
about him being the freshman-of-the-year, we were talking about him
being the national player-of-the-year in college basketball."

Orange fans serenaded him with chants of "One More Year" during
his final games that season in the Carrier Dome in hopes that he would
return. But after earning most outstanding player honors at the Final
Four, Anthony opted to enter the NBA draft and was chosen third overall by the Denver Nuggets in April 2003. "I never for one moment tried
to talk him out of it," Boeheim said. "In my mind, it was the right decision. He was ready to go."

Carmelo Anthony

Date of birth: May 29, 1984

Hometown: Baltimore, Maryland

Honors: Second-team All-America in only season at SU. . . . Bronze
medalist at 2004 Summer Olympics. . . . Most outstanding player of
2003 Final Four. . . . Consensus national freshman of the year. . . .
First-team All–Big East. . . . Made NBA's all-rookie team in 2004.

Achievements: Ranked sixteenth in nation with a 22.2 scoring average
and was nineteenth in nation with 10 rebounds per game. . . . Led
SU to 30-5 record and its only basketball national championship. . . .
Scored in double figures in all 35 of his college games and had 22
double-doubles. . . . Had career-high 33 points against Texas in national semifinals, a Final Four scoring record for a freshman as well
as an SU freshman scoring record.

SU career totals: 778 points, 349 rebounds, 77 assists, 55 steals, 30 blocked
shots.

24

G-Mac Saves the Day

March 19, 2004 *Already one of the most popular players to*
Pepsi Center *ever don a Syracuse uniform, Gerry Mc-*
Denver, Colorado *Namara's Q rating blew through the roof*
when he scored a career-high and Syra-
cuse NCAA Tournament–best 43 points to
single-handedly carry the Orangemen to a
first-round Big Dance victory over BYU.

Talk about a Rocky Mountain high. Nearly a year after drilling six
three-pointers in the first half against Kansas to propel Syracuse to
its first NCAA basketball championship, Gerry McNamara was at it
again, his legend soaring to even greater heights. With the baskets at the
Pepsi Center looking as big to him as hula hoops, the guard known as
G-Mac scored a mind-boggling 43 points to rally the Orangemen to an
80-75 victory against Brigham Young University in the opening round
of the 2003–2004 tournament.

Even those who had become used to such heroics from McNamara
were astounded by the performance that saw him convert nine of eleven
shots from beyond the long distance arc to smash by six the SU record
for most points in an NCAA Tournament game, established by Gary
Clark in 1957. "Just when you think you've seen it all from Gerry . . ."
SU assistant coach Mike Hopkins said afterward, not having to finish
the sentence.

Folks already had seen plenty from McNamara during his freshman
year. Enough, really, to last a lifetime. It took just one season for the
hard-nosed kid from a blue-collar neighborhood in Scranton, Pennsyl-

Gerry McNamara, Syracuse's all-time leading three-point shooter, takes it to the hoop during the 2003 national championship game against Kansas. The following year, McNamara set a school NCAA Tournament record by scoring forty-three points against Brigham Young University.

vania, to establish himself as one of the most popular players in SU's storied hoops history.

It's easy to see why his number 3 jersey quickly became one of the most familiar articles of clothing in the Carrier Dome. Much of McNa-mara's appeal had to do with his scrappy style of play. By frequently diving onto the floor and into the stands for loose balls, he showed he wasn't afraid to leave a little skin and blood on the hardwood in an ef-fort to win. Orange basketball fans took to his infectious, body-be-damned approach.

They also admired his icy demeanor in clutch situations. McNamara absolutely loved having the ball in his hands with the game on the line. He wouldn't hesitate to let it fly, as evidenced by his game-winning shots against Notre Dame and Georgetown and his five points in over-time in an upset of heavily favored Pittsburgh on the road during his sophomore season.

But none of his heroics—not even his bull's-eye marksmanship in the national championship game—could quite match the show he put on in Denver.

There were few indications early on that the six-foot-one, 175-pound guard was going to have the game of his life. In fact, it appeared as if the defending NCAA basketball champs might reach a new low in the Mile High City. They might be one and done. "It was looking pretty bleak there for awhile," Hopkins said.

With BYU leading by eleven midway through the first half and star Syracuse forward Hakim Warrick strapped to the bench with three fouls, some scribes along press row began writing obituaries for the SU basketball season.

Foolish them. The eulogies, on this day, would be written in memory of the BYU basketball season, thanks to McNamara, who added two two-point baskets and twelve free throws to his historic score line. He finished the first half with 28 points as the Orangemen stormed back to tie the score at 42. "He put us on his back and carried us," said Syracuse coach Jim Boeheim. "He knew we were about to go down with a big bang. He knew it was either him or home."

Perhaps the most amazing thing about McNamara's outburst is that he needed just 17 shots to accumulate his 43 points. That's what you call being economical. "Gerry's was as good of a performance as I've seen in college basketball," said Boeheim, who has spent more than four de-cades in the game as a player and a coach and was a teammate of Bas-ketball Hall of Famer Dave Bing. "Gerry was in another world. I don't think we'll see the likes of that kind of game too many times. I can't think of anybody that's put on a performance like that."

It was good that he scored that many points because SU needed virtually every one of them. While McNamara helped the Orangemen climb back into the game with 16 points during the final nine minutes of the first half, Warrick keyed the victory with his second-half spurt. Rested after spending the final seven minutes of the first half on the bench with three fouls, Warrick, a six-foot-eight forward, scored 16 points after intermission. "Hakim said to me at halftime, 'Way to carry us in the first half,' " McNamara said. "And I said, 'It's your turn now.' It was obvious he just took the game over." Not that McNamara took the second half off. Though not as explosive as he had been early on, G-Mac added 15 points after the break.

Despite his barrage, the Orangemen had to sweat it out 'til the very end. The Cougars clawed back to within two, 77-75, and had the ball with thirty seconds remaining. They worked it around and found Mark Bigelow, the school's all-time leading three-point shooter, open just beyond the arc. He let fly with eighteen seconds left, but the ball bounced off the back of the rim and SU rebounded. "I was like, 'Please, please don't make that one,' " Warrick said. "I couldn't believe he was that wide open. Luckily, he didn't knock it down."

Fittingly, McNamara iced the win with three free throws in the final sixteen seconds as the sellout crowd of 19,286 rose in unison to applaud his unforgettable performance.

Obviously, I didn't know I was going to come out and play like that. But from the first shot it just felt good today. I had it rolling. If you're making them, you've got to keep shooting. When you have it, you just have to roll with it. You have to keep throwing it up there.

I'm not Hakim. I'm not going to rise on somebody. I've been a shooter since I was a kid. And today, it was smooth. I kept firing and it felt so good, nothing was going to stop me. I take pride in stepping up in certain situations, and today was one of them. I really felt good about myself because this came at the right time in the best situation.

Hopkins, who had recruited McNamara to come to Syracuse, wasn't totally surprised. He knew the precocious guard had once scored 55 points for Bishop Hannan in a Pennsylvania high school basketball tournament game. "He's one of those players who always seems to play big in big games," Hopkins said.

His growth from high school star to major college star had been both rapid and seamless. "He had the weight of an entire program on his shoulders for four years in high school, so he's had to compete at a high level with a lot of pressure on him," Boeheim said. "There's probably less pressure on him now than there was in high school to be truthful because here he has others who can carry the load."

True enough, but for a good portion of this first-round game against BYU, McNamara put the hopes and dreams of SU's season on his shoulders and didn't quake. In the locker room moments after the Orangemen narrowly escaped the upset, SU center Craig Forth summed up the game with four words: "Thank God for Gerry."

A few weeks after his 43-point barrage in the NCAA Tournament, McNamara discovered the reason he had felt so much pain during the 2003–2004 season. The pulled groin muscle he had suffered midway through the season eventually resulted in a slight stress fracture in his pelvic bone that wasn't discovered until he went for postseason X rays. The injury explained why McNamara would feel a shock shoot up and down his left leg each time he made a lateral move or landed on it after a jump shot. The son of a Marine Corps sergeant, McNamara refused to take any time off during the season because point guard Billy Edelin had left the Orangemen for personal reasons and he didn't want to leave his team in the lurch. So he gutted it out through SU's final game in mid-March. His gritty performance under the circumstances merely added to the legend of G-Mac.

Orange Slice—Hakim Warrick

The most memorable—and most painful—moment in Syracuse hoops history used to be the Keith Smart jumper that deprived the Orangemen of a national basketball championship at the Louisiana Superdome in 1987. But sixteen years later in the very same building that Indiana out-Smarted the Orange, Hakim Warrick erased a shot and those heart-breaking memories.

With 1.5 seconds remaining and Kansas staging a furious comeback

Hakim Warrick is one of only three players in Syracuse history—Derrick Coleman and John Wallace are the others—who rank in the top ten in both career scoring and rebounding.

in the 2003 NCAA title game, Warrick came from far away and rejected a potential game-tying three-pointer by Michael Lee. The stunning block preserved SU's first-ever NCAA basketball championship and gave Orange hoop fans a moment to savor rather than dread.

Though that block is the seminal moment of Warrick's SU career, it is hardly the only one. In his four seasons with the Orangemen, the lean six-foot-eight forward with the long, elastic arms and incredible leaping ability continually thrilled fans and teammates with his highlight-reel dunks. "It's as if he has wings," guard Gerry McNamara said of the teammate who became known to Carrier Dome fans as "the Philadelphia Flyer." "He defies the laws of gravity."

Playing for a small high school outside of Philadelphia, Warrick flew under the recruiting radar screen. Many coaches believed he was too skinny to perform in a rough-and-tumble league like the Big East Conference, but Boeheim thought otherwise. He focused on Warrick's remarkable reach and athleticism rather than his paper-thin physique. Boeheim saw something in Warrick that others missed. That potential wound up being realized as Warrick blossomed into the league's player of the year by his senior year. He finished his four-year career ranked number four in SU history in both points and rebounds, one of only three players in school history to rank in the top five in both categories, Derrick Coleman and John Wallace being the others.

But he will always be remembered for the block he made in the national championship game. It became the signature play in SU hoops history.

Hakim Warrick

Date of birth: July 8, 1982

Hometown: Philadelphia, Pennsylvania

Honors: Two-time All-American including first-team selection in 2005. . . . Two-time first team All–Big East. . . . 2005 Big East player of the year.

Achievements: Completed his SU career ranked fourth all-time in both scoring and rebounding. . . . His 310 free-throw attempts in 2004–2005 were an SU single-season record, and his 211 made free throws were the third-highest total. . . . His 726 points as a senior were the sixth-highest single-season total in school history. . . . Led team in both scoring and rebounding his final two years.

SU career totals: 2,073 points, 1,025 rebounds, 128 blocked shots, 131 steals.

25

A Patriotic Victory

May 31, 2004
M&T Bank Stadium
Baltimore, Maryland

There was no question who the sentimental favorite was, but Syracuse—cast in the role of the Evil Empire—nonetheless overcame a partisan and jingoistic crowd and spoiled Navy's dream season. By preventing the Midshipmen from winning the 2004 lacrosse national championship game, the Orangemen increased their collection of national titles to an unprecedented nine.

Syracuse long-stick defenseman Dan DiPietro noticed it as he watched Navy play Princeton in the first national semifinal of the 2004 NCAA Division I lacrosse tournament at M&T Bank Stadium. "When Princeton scored, like six people clapped," DiPietro said with a smile that lent credence to his exaggeration.

More than six people clapped for the Tigers that sun-splashed afternoon on the banks of Chesapeake Bay, but there weren't too many more among the all-time tournament record crowd of 46,923 who were rooting for Princeton in its game against Navy. And when the Midshipmen completed a somewhat surprising 8-7 victory that advanced them to the national championship game for a meeting with Syracuse, another hugely partisan crowd of 43,898 spent a rainy Memorial Day afternoon cheering not so much against the Orangemen, but for Navy.

The Midshipmen were one of the great stories of 2004, on the playing field as well as the battlefield. Navy's lacrosse team had not played for

In 2004 Mike Powell surpassed his brothers Casey and Ryan to become Syracuse's all-time leading scorer with 307 points. In the process he led the Orangemen to their ninth lacrosse national championship.

the national championship since 1975 and hadn't won it outright since 1966, five years before the birth of the NCAA Tournament. And now, in a dramatic year when the young men and women of our armed forces—many of whom were classmates of the members of Navy's team—were overseas fighting for our way of life in Iraq and Afghanistan, here were the Midshipmen, fighting a battle not of life and death but of pride and athletic achievement.

Besides the cluster of a few thousand orange-clad Syracuse fans, everyone wanted Navy to win, and this was not lost on the Orangemen. "Steve [Vallone] just read the article in *The Baltimore Sun*, the Navy article, and he said, 'Geez, I almost want Navy to win,' " Syracuse attackman Mike Powell quipped the day before the showdown for lacrosse supremacy, the day after the Orangemen defeated number one–ranked Johns Hopkins, 15-9, to make it to their mind-boggling fourteenth title game in twenty-two years. "It's kind of weird," Vallone said. "We've never been in a situation like this where we're kind of like the Evil Empire going against our own government. It's crazy playing against a team that everybody's rooting for."

But that was Syracuse's task, and the preeminent lacrosse program in the nation rose above the jingoism and delivered to Orange Nation a record ninth NCAA Championship with a thrilling 14-13 victory over sentimental favorite Navy. "Today was very emotional," said Syracuse head coach John Desko. "This game was a very different championship game, because of our opponent. The United States Naval Academy, [coach] Richie Meade and his staff just had a real sense of pride. I was so proud of them being there and the way they played all season. They played with a bigger cause and to go out and play them, it didn't have the feel of a typical opponent. We were pulling for them as well."

Just not during those wonderful sixty minutes when Syracuse answered every challenge Navy set forth. "I'm real happy," said Powell, the tournament's most outstanding player who closed his Syracuse career with 150 goals and 157 assists for a school record 307 points. "We were playing a lacrosse team. A lot of people took it a little too far. We weren't playing to beat our country; we weren't playing to beat the Naval Academy. It was just another opponent that we had to face. We didn't view it as something unpatriotic. We viewed it as national championship game, and I think that was the right mindset to approach the game with, and we carried it throughout the game."

And what a game it was. It was dramatic theater from the opening face-off, the lead and momentum changing hands on several occasions, the score tied no less than ten times, and as the clock wound down it looked as if the script was calling for the ultimate Cinderella ending.

200 I Slices of Orange

The Midshipmen, winners of 15 of their first 17 games during an improbable rebound from 2003 when they went 6-7 and failed to qualify for the NCAA Tournament, forged ahead 12-11 with 5:40 left to play when Clipper Lennon fired a shot past Syracuse goalie Jay Pfeifer.

Powell, considered by many to be the finest college lacrosse player ever, surpassing even his older brothers, Casey and Ryan, and another set of brothers who starred on the hill, Gary Gait and Paul Gait, had another ending in mind. Remember, this was his last collegiate game, his swan song, his final moment to bask in the glory, and according to the script he intended on following, Cinderella wasn't getting to the ball. More precisely, Navy wasn't getting to that loose ball near midfield, the loose ball that ultimately cemented the victory for Syracuse.

Goals by Brian Crockett and Brian Nee sent the Orangemen back into the lead at 13-12 with 3:37 remaining, and after a couple tense minutes of back-and-forth but scoreless action, a Navy mistake set the stage for Powell to, er, exit. An errant Navy pass wound up on the turf near the center stripe, and Nee—a Baltimore native who had a few people cheering for him—swooped in to retrieve it and took off on a two-on-one break with Powell. Nee whipped a perfect pass to his best friend, and Powell, who had been held without a goal through the first 59 minutes, bounced a shot past Navy backup goalie Colin Finnegan with 60 seconds to go to make it 14-12. "When it first happened, I was just excited I finally scored because their goalie owned me today," said Powell.

Of course, that goalie had been Matt Russell, Navy's gritty netminder who had been so instrumental in the Middies reaching this point. However, Russell had to leave the championship game with 8 minutes left because of a shoulder injury, and the inexperienced Finnegan was between the pipes during the game's frenetic closing stretch. "To end my career scoring the last goal and to win by one in the national championship game, I mean, Hollywood should buy that," said Powell. Especially considering what happened in those final 60 seconds.

Navy's Chris Pieczonka of Skaneateles won the ensuing face-off, and within 20 seconds the Midshipmen were back within one, 14-13, when Ian Dingman, a Carthage native who was a high school teammate of Powell, muscled his way through the Syracuse defense to beat Pfeifer. And then Pieczonka won another face-off, and the Middies were on the attack again as Pieczonka scooped the loose ball himself and ran down the middle of the field toward the Syracuse net.

Just as he was about to uncork a shot, Syracuse's Jarrett Park checked his stick, and the ball flew harmlessly over Pfeifer's head and out-of-bounds with 31 seconds left. "It looked like he was going to the goal," Park said, "and I just laid out for him hoping I was going to get it." Syracuse was one successful clear away from celebrating.

Not so fast, destiny said. With 13 seconds to go Navy was awarded the ball at midfield thanks to a goalie-interference infraction. Time for one last shot. "You just take a couple deep breaths, relax and realize that the ball's coming down and you've got to make a big save," said Pfeifer. "You just try to concentrate on the ball."

Pfeifer need not have worried. He made 15 saves in the game, but none in this final sequence. Navy midfielder Graham Gill took the ball and tried to pass to the crease area, but Orange midfielder Kevin Dougherty intercepted and then heaved the ball out of harm's way to the other end of the field as the clock struck zero, or in the case of Navy midnight. "He just threw the ball right to me," Dougherty said.

It was expected that Navy, one of the best defensive teams in the country, would try to slow the pace of the game, fearful of getting into a run-and-gun affair with a Syracuse team that thrived on that style. Instead, the Middies came out smoking and matched the Orangemen goal for goal, and when the first quarter ended it was 4-4 as eight different players scored. Skaneateles's Joe Bossi put Navy ahead just 13 seconds into the second period, the Orangemen answered with three in a row in a four-minute span including two by Nee, only to see Dingman and Ben Horn score for Navy to produce a 7-7 halftime tie. Goals by Vallone, Crockett, and Alex Zink enabled the Orangemen to take a 10-8 lead into the fourth quarter, but Navy refused to buckle. "Four or five times they had a chance to pull away from us, but we always fought back," said Meade. Horn, Joe Birsner, and Bossi scored in the first five minutes to send Navy back into an 11-10 lead, and after Sean Lindsay scored while Syracuse was enjoying a two-man advantage, Lennon gave the Midshipmen their final lead at 12-11.

Most in the huge crowd sighed a groan of disappointment when the game ended, but it sounded like a lot more than six people were clapping for Syracuse's victory, a victory so fitting for the departing seniors, particularly Powell. "I had a lot of things going through my mind," said Powell, who immediately after graduation shunned an opportunity to continue his lacrosse career in the professional ranks.

> Ever since I was a kid, I'd dreamed of getting the goal that won the championship. And after all this time it finally came true. Scoring the last goal of the season. Scoring the last goal of my career. Scoring the game-winning goal. There's nothing better than that.
>
> In the lacrosse world, this is as big as I'll ever be. It's tough to know that it won't ever be better for me than what's going on right now. That's one reason why I want to get out.

While Powell, who reconsidered and did play professionally in 2005 for the Baltimore Bayhawks of Major League Lacrosse, had a choice in regards to what he was going to do with his post-Syracuse life, the graduating seniors from Navy's team did not. It was on to a life in the military, where many would be put in harm's way fighting for the freedom of Powell and the rest of us. "It was a great honor playing here today," said Dingman. "Every lacrosse team in the country wanted to be playing today. Playing on Memorial Day and being in the military is extra special. Honoring our veterans in all the wars, I hope they aren't anything but proud of us."

It was another magical day for the Orange, but this one was tinged with sadness. As soon as the final gun sounded and the Syracuse sideline erupted in celebration, the end—at least for now—of the Powell era became a reality.

Orange Slice—The Powell Brothers

In the winter of 2005 Mason Powell of Carthage turned eleven years old, and already there are kids asking for his autograph. He gladly obliges and adds the number 22 to his signature. The waiting has begun at Syracuse for Mason, youngest of the four lacrosse-playing Powell brothers.

The graduation of Mike in the spring of 2004 meant that for the first time in ten years the Orange lacrosse team took the field in 2005 without a Powell on the roster.

Casey began the parade from Carthage in 1995 when he boldly took

The 2005 season was the first in more than a decade when Syracuse did not have one of the Powell brothers on its roster. From left to right, Casey, Mike, and Ryan combined for 881 points during their careers.

the number 22 jersey that had been held in such high esteem ever since Gary Gait wore it during his four fabulous years at Syracuse and was kept ably warm by Charlie Lockwood in the early 1990s. All Casey did was score a school record 287 points, earn All-American recognition four times, win two Division I player of the year awards, and help the Orangemen win the 1995 national championship. "He did a lot of things with either hand that you wouldn't have seen before unless you had seen Paul and Gary Gait," said coach Roy Simmons Jr., who recruited Casey, coached him all four years, then retired following Casey's final game in 1998.

Along came Ryan in 1997 and after wearing number 1 until Casey moved on, Ryan assumed the number 22 in 1999 and did it proud. He tied Casey's all-time record for points—appropriately enough in the final game of his career when he led the Orangemen to the 2000 national championship, the same year he was voted player of the year and, like Casey, earned his All-American recognition for the fourth year.

On that emotional day at College Park, Maryland, when Ryan scored his 287th point in Hollywood-style fashion with an assist just eighteen seconds before the conclusion of Syracuse's 13-7 championship-game victory over Princeton, he took off the jersey, handed it to Mike, and said, "I'm old news. You're the new No. 22."

Both Casey and Ryan said Mike would be the best Powell yet, and they were right. He set the new scoring standard for young Mason to aspire to by scoring 307 points, and he became the first Powell to win two championships and earn first-team All-American honors four times. "The reason I recruited Casey and Ryan is so I could get Mike," Simmons joked one time, even though it was Simmons's replacement, John Desko, who closed the deal on bringing Mike to Syracuse in 2001.

Together the Powell brothers combined for 445 goals, 881 points, four NCAA championships, nine first-team All-American selections, five NCAA player of the year awards, and six attackman of the year awards. The Powells have a lacrosse lineage that defies description, and young Mason has quite a challenge in front of him when he gets to Syracuse—assuming he follows in his brothers' footsteps—along about 2012.

"It's not the end of an era," Casey told Donna Ditota of the Syracuse *Post-Standard* in 2004 when he, Ryan, and Michael sat down for a Q&A. "There's going to be a little pause in it, but there's another one, and hopefully he can accomplish some of the things that we have."

Casey Powell

Date of birth: February 18, 1976

Hometown: Carthage, New York

Honors: Four-time All-American including three first-team selections. . . . 1998 Turnbull Award winner as nation's best attackman. . . . Two-time NCAA player of the year. . . . Four-time NCAA all-tournament team selection.

Achievements: Held SU's all-time career points record when he graduated in 1998. . . . Scored 45 points in NCAA Tournament games, tied for fourth best in school history. . . . Holds the school record for most points in a game with 13. . . . Was named to the *Lacrosse Magazine* all-century team.

SU career totals: 158 goals, 129 assists, 287 points.

Ryan Powell

Date of birth: February 23, 1978

Hometown: Carthage, New York

Honors: Four-time All-American including two first-team selections. . . . 2000 Turnbull Award winner as nation's top attackman. . . . Was 2000 NCAA player of the year. . . . Three-time NCAA all-tournament team selection.

Achievements: Tied for the number-one spot on SU's all-time scoring list when he graduated in 2000. . . . Ranks third in SU history with 24 NCAA Tournament assists. . . . Scored 18 points during 2000 NCAA Tournament. . . . Scored 96 points in 2000, tied for second-best season in SU history.

SU career totals: 137 goals, 150 assists, 287 points.

Michael Powell

Date of birth: October 29, 1982

Hometown: Carthage, New York

Honors: SU's only four-time first-team All-American. . . . Two-time winner of the Tewaaraton Trophy as nation's best player, the equivalent of the Heisman Trophy. . . . Four-time Turnbull Award winner as nation's best attackman. . . . Two-time NCAA Tournament MVP.

Achievements: Is SU's all-time leading scorer with 307 points. . . . Led SU in scoring all four years he played. . . . Only Powell brother to play on two NCAA Championship–winning teams.

SU career totals: 150 goals, 157 assists, 307 points.

Appendix

• • •

Bibliography

APPENDIX

Other Games Not to Be Forgotten

Football

November 23, 1889—Syracuse played its first varsity football game, and wearing pink and blue uniforms it was trounced, 36-0, by the University of Rochester.

November 7, 1891—With six hundred fans looking on at rock-strewn Star Park in Syracuse, Colgate scored a 22-16 victory to kick off one of eastern football's most colorful rivalries.

November 5, 1904—On a cold, rainy day, Syracuse scored its most decisive football victory, crushing visiting Manhattan College, 144-0, at the Old Oval on the SU campus. Coach Charles P. Hutchins's Orangemen scored twenty-five touchdowns and did not allow its opponent to gain a single yard or first down. Mercifully, the game was called on account of darkness.

September 25, 1907—The Orangemen christened brand-new Archbold Stadium with a 28-0 victory against Hobart College. Bill Horr, SU's first football All-American, led the way with a seventy-five-yard touchdown run.

November 18, 1911—SU's powerful defense stymied the great Jim Thorpe as the Orangemen upset Carlisle, 12-11, in a decision that one scribe labeled a "miracle."

November 13, 1915—Led by its "Big Four" of T. R. Johnson, Babe White, Chris Schlachter, and Ty Cobb, Syracuse throttled rival Colgate, 38-0. It would be one of nine shutouts by the Orangemen, who would go 9-1-2 but decline a Rose Bowl invitation.

October 18, 1919—Coach Buck O'Neill's Orangemen squashed Pittsburgh, 24-3, to hand the visiting Panthers their first loss in four seasons. Afterward, losing coach Pop Warner called SU "the best and fastest eleven of all-time."

November 4, 1922—A few weeks after defeating Notre Dame and its famed Four Horsemen, Nebraska was upset 9-6 by the Orangemen at Archbold Stadium. Tackle Lynn "Pappy" Waldorf, who would gain fame as a coach, sparked the upset of the team that some had heralded as the best of all time. Swede Anderson scored the winning touchdown on a five-yard run in the fourth quarter.

November 5, 1938—Phil Allen scored on an end around from fourteen yards out as Syracuse snapped a thirteen-year losing streak against upstate rival Colgate at Archbold. SU fans were so excited they tore down the goalposts. Thousands of them filled the streets of downtown Syracuse in the biggest celebration the city has witnessed other than the one that marked the end of World War II.

January 15, 1953—Playing in its first bowl game, Syracuse was crushed, 61-6, by Alabama in the Orange Bowl. The Tide gained 586 yards on offense, and its defense forced seven turnovers. Syracuse's only score came on a Pat Stark–to–Joe Szombathy pass in the first quarter.

January 1, 1957—In Jim Brown's final game in an Orange uniform, the bruising back rushed for 132 yards and scored three touchdowns and three conversions, but Syracuse lost a heartbreaking 28-27 decision to TCU in the Cotton Bowl.

January 1, 1959—Syracuse's bowl woes continued as it lost its third straight, 21-6 to Oklahoma in the Orange Bowl. Syracuse actually outgained Bud Wilkinson's team 311-245 but was done in by three turnovers and Brewster Hobby, who threw a 79-yard touchdown pass and returned a punt 40 yards for another score.

November 7, 1959—Roger Kochman was stopped short of the goal line on his two-point conversion attempt as the visiting Orangemen withstood a furious Penn State rally to win 20-18. The victory preserved the Orangemen's perfect season. It proved to be their only close call en route to an 11-0 record.

December 16, 1961—Ernie Davis capped his Heisman Trophy season by rushing for 140 yards and one touchdown as SU rallied from a 14-0 deficit to defeat Miami, 15-14, in the Liberty Bowl. Dave Sarette threw for 148 yards and hit Dick Easterly with a game-winning 7-yard TD pass in the fourth quarter.

January 1, 1965—Despite the two-headed rushing monster of Floyd Little and Jim Nance combining for 116 yards, Syracuse could not overcome LSU and lost 13-10 in the Sugar Bowl. The Orange led 10-2 in the third quarter before Billy Ezell hit Doug Moreau with a 57-yard TD pass and then passed to Joe Labruzzo for the tying two-point conversion. Moreau then won the game for LSU with a 28-yard field goal with 3:50 left to play.

December 31, 1966—Floyd Little closed out his Syracuse career with a Gator Bowl–record 216 yards rushing, and Larry Csonka ran for 114 yards, but the Orange still lost, 18-12, to Tennessee. The Vols raced out to an 18-0 halftime lead, and touchdowns by Csonka in the third quarter and Little late in the fourth left SU one score short.

November 25, 1967—Syracuse closed an 8-2 season by traveling out to Los Angeles where it pummeled UCLA, the nation's fourth-ranked team, 32-14. A week earlier the Bruins had won a showdown against number one–ranked USC and O. J. Simpson, 21-10, at the Los Angeles Coliseum, one of the most famous games in college football history. But UCLA had nothing left against the Orange as Bruins quarterback Gary Beban—who took home the Heisman Trophy a few weeks later—was held to three completions in eleven pass attempts for just 17 yards, and he had minus-9 yards rushing on nine carries before being knocked out of the game with an injury in the third quarter. In the final game of his SU career Larry Csonka, who finished fourth in the Heisman balloting, rushed for 59 yards and a touchdown while quarterback Rick Cassata passed for 146, ran for 119, and was responsible for four TDs.

October 30, 1976—Eventual Heisman Trophy winner Tony Dorsett of Pittsburgh rushed for 241 yards on thirty-four carries, at the time the highest rushing yield to an opponent in Syracuse history, but the Orange battled gamely against the nation's number two–ranked team and almost pulled a major upset before losing, 23-13.

September 24, 1977—Despite 257 yards passing by University of Washington quarterback Warren Moon, the Orange pulled off a 22-20 upset over a Huskies team that ultimately won the Pacific-8 Conference, defeated number-four Michigan in the Rose Bowl, and finished number ten in the final polls. Bill Hurley rushed for 113 yards and led a drive to Dave Jacobs's game-winning 31-yard field goal with twenty-three seconds remaining.

November 5, 1977—During a 45-34 victory over Navy at Annapolis, Maryland, Syracuse wingback Art Monk set a school record by catching fourteen passes totaling 188 yards.

October 6, 1979—Joe Morris set the SU all-time single-game rushing record when he gained 252 yards on just twenty-three carries during a 45-27 victory at Kansas.

December 15, 1979—Making a return to the bowl scene for the first time in thirteen years, the Orange crushed lightly regarded McNeese State, 31-7, in the Independence Bowl. Joe Morris rushed for 155 yards, and in the final games of their careers Bill Hurley and Art Monk hooked up on a 9-yard touchdown pass.

November 7, 1981—Eddie Meyers of the Naval Academy shredded the Orange for 298 rushing yards and four touchdowns in a 25-23 Midshipman victory. His rushing total remains the most ever allowed by an Orange team. Only a few weeks earlier, Penn State's Curt Warner had set the previous record with a 256-yard output during a 41-16 Nittany Lion victory.

November 16, 1985—In the midst of a five-game winning streak, the Orange outlasted Boston College at the Dome, 41-21. That day Scott Schwedes set an SU record with 249 receiving yards, and BC quarterback Shawn Halloran passed for 453 yards, a record total against the Orange that lasted seventeen years.

December 21, 1985—Dick MacPherson's first bowl game as Syracuse coach was the Cherry Bowl in the Pontiac Silverdome, and the result was a 35-18 loss to Maryland. Quarterback Don McPherson produced 315 yards in total offense, and Robert Drummond rushed for 93 yards and a touchdown, but Maryland scored 22 points in the second quarter to put the game away.

January 1, 1988—Syracuse brought an 11-0 record and number-four national ranking into the Sugar Bowl, but saw its dreams of a perfect season and outside chance of a national championship dashed when Auburn rallied for a 16-16 tie. SU led 16-13, but Tigers coach Pat Dye elected to kick a tying field goal rather than go for the victory. Win Lyle made the 30-yard attempt, and Orange coach Dick MacPherson was livid. Don McPherson passed for 140 yards and threw a touchdown pass to Deval Glover, and Tim Vesling kicked three field goals for Syracuse.

January 2, 1989—In his only season as the starting quarterback, Todd Philcox led the Orange to a 10-2 record, capped by a 23-10 victory over LSU in the Hall of Fame Bowl. SU broke away from a 10-10 third-quarter tie with a pair of impressive scoring drives that ended with Robert Drummond's short TD plunge and Philcox's TD pass to Deval Glover. Drummond led the Orange with 122 yards rushing.

December 30, 1989—Bill Scharr's lone season as the starting quarterback ended with an exciting 19-18 victory over Georgia in the Peach Bowl. John Biskup's 26-yard field goal with twenty-five seconds remaining capped a Syracuse rally from an 18-7 third-quarter deficit. After Scharr threw 3 interceptions, Mark McDonald replaced him and passed for 135 yards, including a TD pass to Rob Moore that pulled the Orange within striking distance.

December 25, 1990—Syracuse traveled all the way to Hawaii on Christmas Day and made the trip worthwhile with a 28-0 spanking of Arizona in the Aloha Bowl in Dick MacPherson's last game as coach. Marvin Graves produced 190 yards of total offense and threw two touchdown passes and rushed for two other scores, while the SU defense dealt the Wildcats their first shutout in nineteen years.

September 21, 1991—The seventeenth-ranked Orange opened their game at the Dome against fifth-ranked Florida with some razzle-dazzle. They tried a reverse on the opening kickoff, the play completely fooled Steve Spurrier's Gators, and Kirby Dar Dar raced 95 yards for a touchdown. Syracuse never looked back and rolled to a 38-21 victory. The SU defense held Florida to minus-17 yards rushing, though Gators QB Shane Matthews did pass for 347 yards.

January 1, 1992—Syracuse scored the first two times it touched the ball and took a 14-0 lead, allowed Ohio State to tie the game in the fourth quarter, then pulled out a 24-17 victory in the Hall of Fame Bowl. Marvin Graves passed for a career-high 309 yards in outdueling current ESPN college football analyst Kirk Herbstreit. Graves threw a 50-yard TD pass to Shelby Hill in the first quarter and a game-winning 60-yard TD pass to Antonio Johnson.

October 10, 1992—Marvin Graves set all-time single-game SU records for passing yards (425) and total offensive yards (476) during a 50-28 rout of Rutgers at the Dome.

January 1, 1993—Earning his third straight bowl game MVP award, Marvin Graves scored on a 28-yard run, and Kirby Dar Dar returned a third-quarter kickoff 100 yards for a clinching touchdown as the Orange defeated Colorado, 26-22, in the Fiesta Bowl. Syracuse's defense, led by Dan Conley and Glen Young who combined for twenty-three tackles, picked off three Kordell Stewart passes.

January 1, 1996—The Orange raced to a 20-0 first-quarter lead and never looked back in blowing out Clemson, 41-0, in a rainy Gator Bowl. Donovan McNabb made his bowl-game debut and passed for 309 yards and three touchdowns and also ran for a score. Marvin Harrison closed out his SU career with seven catches for 173 yards and two TDs.

December 27, 1996—Syracuse stretched its bowl-game winning streak to seven with a 30-17 triumph over Houston in the Liberty Bowl. Malcolm Thomas rushed for 201 yards, second most by a Syracuse back in a bowl game, and the Orange finished with 396 yards on the ground as Donovan McNabb added 49 yards and two rushing touchdowns.

December 31, 1997—The Orange lost in a bowl game for the first time since 1985 as Kansas State rolled to a 35-18 victory behind its outstanding quarterback, Michael Bishop, who threw for 317 yards and four touchdowns in outgunning Donovan McNabb (271 yards passing, 81 yards rushing).

January 2, 1999—Donovan McNabb closed out his fabulous career on a downer as Steve Spurrier's Florida Gators routed Syracuse, 31-10, in the Orange Bowl. SU held the ball nearly eleven minutes in the first quarter but found itself trailing 14-0 thanks to a pair of Doug Johnson TD passes to Travis Taylor, and the Orange never recovered. McNabb passed for 192 yards and a 62-yard touchdown to Maurice Jackson, but Syracuse committed four turnovers.

December 29, 1999—The Orange fell behind 10-0 to Kentucky in the Music City Bowl, but rallied for two touchdowns in the fourth quarter to pull out a 20-13 victory. James Mungro's 86-yard run set up a TD by Kyle Johnson in the second quarter, and then Mungro scored on runs of 32 and 20 yards, the second coming with 1:42 left to play. Mungro finished with 162 yards rushing.

December 29, 2001—James Mungro rushed for 117 yards and three touchdowns including a 65-yard jaunt in the first quarter to lead the Orange to a 26-3 rout of Kansas State in the Insight.Com Bowl. Despite the lopsided score, the SU offense managed only eight first downs, but the defense held the Wildcats to 33 rushing yards on thirty-four attempts, and Willie Ford had two interceptions.

November 9, 2002—With Troy Nunes becoming only the second player in SU history to surpass 400 yards passing in a game, an Orange team that would finish at 4-8, the worst record of the Paul Pasqualoni era, pulled out a thrilling 50-42 victory in triple overtime over seventh-ranked Virginia Tech at the Dome. That day, Hokies quarterback Bryan Randall set the record for most yards passing against Syracuse when he threw for 504 and five touchdowns.

December 6, 2003—With Notre Dame making its first visit to the Dome and its first trip to Syracuse since 1914, a sellout crowd looking to salvage a disappointing season was treated to a 38-12 rout of the Irish. Walter Reyes rushed for 189 yards and five touchdowns to become the all-time record holder for rushing TDs in a season (twenty-one).

December 21, 2004—One of Syracuse's worst performances in a bowl game occurred in the Champs Sports Bowl when the Orange were embarrassed by Georgia Tech, 51-14, in Paul Pasqualoni's last game as head coach. Three touchdowns in a span of 3:09 in the second quarter spelled doom for the Orange as the Yellow Jackets took a 35-6 lead into halftime.

Basketball

December 29, 1925—In what is considered the best all-around game of his magnificent career, Vic Hanson scored 25 points in a 30-25 overtime victory over Pennsylvania.

January 8, 1927—The Orange lost in overtime to Pittsburgh, 29-28, the only home game the team lost during the three-year varsity career of Vic Hanson.

March 3, 1948—Billy Gabor, to this point the all-time leading Syracuse scorer, played his final college home game for Syracuse and scored 25 points in a 72-59 victory over Niagara. Gabor would go on to play seven seasons in the NBA with the Syracuse Nationals.

March 12, 1957—The Orange made their NCAA Tournament debut in the East Region at Madison Square Garden, and after falling behind by 12 points they rallied to defeat Connecticut, 82-76.

March 16, 1957—Having reached the Elite Eight, Syracuse's first NCAA Tournament run ended when it lost, 67-58, to North Carolina. Some believe SU might have won had Jim Brown played basketball that season as he had the previous two years. The Tar Heels went on to defeat the Wilt Chamberlain–led Kansas Jayhawks in the national championship game.

March 3, 1962—One night after Wilt Chamberlain of the Philadelphia Warriors scored 100 points in an NBA game against the New York Knicks, SU snapped its school-record twenty-seven-game losing streak with a 73-72 victory at Boston College. The Orange lost the final five games of the 1960–1961 season, then began the 1961–1962 season 0-22.

December 28, 1965—Syracuse traveled out to Los Angeles to play in the Los Angeles Classic, and in a first-round game Dave Bing scored a school-record 46 points and outgunned Vanderbilt All-American forward Clyde Lee who had 39 points and 24 rebounds. However, the Commodores won the game, 113-98.

February 14, 1966—During a season in which the Orange averaged 99 points per game and topped 100 points on fourteen occasions, this was the high-water night, a 125-105 victory at Colgate. It was the fifth-highest single-game output in school history. Dave Bing had 35 points, 12 rebounds, and 9 assists; Rick Dean chipped in 30 points; and Jim Boeheim had a quiet game with 4 points.

December 7, 1968—Niagara's Calvin Murphy erupted for 68 points to lead the Purple Eagles to a 118-110 victory over the Orange in Niagara Falls. It is the most points ever scored by an opposing player against SU.

January 14, 1971—Bill Smith set the school single-game scoring record with 47 points in a 106-92 victory over Lafayette at Manley Field House.

February 22, 1971—Julius Erving of Massachusetts, later to be known as Dr. J during his Hall of Fame ABA and NBA careers, pulled down 32 rebounds to lead the Minutemen to an 86-71 victory over SU, the most rebounds ever by an opposing individual against the Orange.

January 8, 1972—One of the keys to Syracuse securing a bid to the NIT Tournament was an 86-83 upset of number-seventeen St. John's at Alumni Hall. Greg Kohls scored 33 points, including the Orange's last 10.

March 29, 1975—In their first appearance in the Final Four, the Orange were bounced in the national semifinals by Kentucky, 95-79, in San Diego. Jack Givens had 24 points and 11 rebounds for Kentucky.

March 13, 1977—In the first round of the NCAA Tournament in Baton Rouge, Louisiana, the Orange knocked off favored Tennessee, 93-88, in overtime, a Vols team that was led by Bernard King and Ernie Grunfeld. That day the Louie and Bouie Show overshadowed the Ernie and Bernie Show.

March 16, 1980—Just three days after seeing their fifty-seven-game home-court winning streak at Manley Field House snapped, the Orange hit the road to play St. John's at Alumni Hall and came away with a 72-71 victory that clinched the first Big East Conference regular-season title. Hal Cohen made a steal in the waning seconds and fed Louis Orr for the winning basket.

March 25, 1981—After winning the Big East Conference Tournament on their home floor, the Orange were snubbed by the NCAA Tournament at a time when the Big East winner did not receive an automatic bid. SU bounced back and won four straight games in the NIT Tournament before losing the championship game at Madison Square Garden to Tulsa, 86-84, in overtime.

January 10, 1983—Leo Rautins recorded the first triple-double in Big East history with 12 points, 13 rebounds, and 10 assists in a 97-92 loss to Georgetown. In the first ten years of the Big East there were only three triple-doubles, and Rautins produced two within a month's time during his senior season.

December 4, 1983—Gene Waldron set the all-time Dome scoring record when he erupted for 40 points during a 109-92 victory over Iona.

March 8, 1986—The eighth-ranked Orange lost a 70-69 decision to number-five St. John's in the championship game of the Big East Tournament. Walter Berry blocked Pearl Washington's game-winning shot attempt as the buzzer sounded, yet Pearl was still named the tournament MVP. Two days earlier Pearl had scored 28 points to lead a 75-73 victory over Georgetown.

March 16, 1986—During the second round of the NCAA Tournament, despite playing at the Dome, Syracuse was upset by Navy, 97-85. David Robinson set Orange opponent NCAA Tournament records for free throws attempted (27) and made (21) and blocked shots (7), and he scored 35 points to tie a mark held by Kansas State's Chuckie Williams that was set in 1975.

March 21, 1987—With Rony Seikaly scoring 26 points and grabbing 11 rebounds, the Orange knocked off Dean Smith and North Carolina, 79-75, in the East Regional final of the NCAA Tournament, securing the first Final Four berth for Jim Boeheim.

January 28, 1989—Sherman Douglas set an NCAA record by dishing out 22 assists in a 100-96 victory over Providence at the Dome.

February 28, 1989—Sherman Douglas broke Dave Bing's Syracuse career scoring record, and he became the NCAA's all-time assist king during an 88-72 romp over Connecticut at the Dome. The home crowd flung records and CDs onto the court to mark the occasion.

March 14, 1991—Syracuse's darkest moment in an NCAA Tournament occurred when it became the first number-two seed since the expansion to the sixty-four-team tournament to lose to a number-fifteen seed as Richmond pulled off a 73-69 victory at Cole Field House in Maryland.

March 24, 1994—During a 98-88 overtime loss to Missouri in the Sweet 16 of the NCAA Tournament, Adrian Autry set a school tournament record for points in a half with 31. Missouri's 98 points were the most SU has ever allowed in a tournament game.

December 23, 1995—Playing at Arizona's McHale Center where the Wildcats had a record of 123-6 since the 1987–1988 season with just one loss in a nonconference game, the Orange handed them number two. With John Wallace scoring 26 points and grabbing 9 rebounds, SU defeated Lute Olsen's third-ranked team, 79-70.

March 22, 1996—After Jason Cipolla had hit a buzzer beater to tie the score and send the game into overtime, John Wallace won the Sweet 16 game against Georgia, 83-81, with a buzzer-beating three-pointer, giving him 30 points for the night.

January 24, 2000—In the midst of a 19-0 start to the season, the fourth-ranked Orange used a 22-2 run in the first half to blow out defending national champion and sixth-ranked UConn, 88-74. Six players scored in double figures, led by Ryan Blackwell's 18.

February 1, 2003—On what may have been the night that SU fans began thinking something special was on the horizon, second-ranked Pittsburgh came to town and lost to the Orange, 67-65. Jeremy McNeil sank two free throws to tie the game, then, after a Carmelo Anthony steal, McNeil scored off the rebound of a Gerry McNamara miss with three seconds left for the victory.

February 29, 2004—Third-ranked Pittsburgh's forty-game home-court winning streak came to an end, and the Panthers suffered their first loss ever at the Petersen Events Center, which had opened in 2002. SU captured a 49-46 overtime victory as Gerry McNamara hit a go-ahead three-pointer and then made two free throws with twenty-seven seconds left to seal the victory.

February 5, 2005—In front of the largest on-campus crowd in NCAA basketball history, 33,199 at the Dome—Syracuse rallied from a 50-39 deficit with 6:05 left to play to overtake Notre Dame, 60-57. Gerry McNamara scored 18 of his 22 points in the second half and made all 11 of his free throws.

February 26, 2005—Playing in his final home game, Hakim Warrick scored a career-high 36 points to lead the Orange to a 91-66 victory over

Providence, as Jim Boeheim recorded the seven hundredth win of his career, just the eighteenth coach in history to reach that plateau.

Lacrosse

May 18, 1957—The Orange defeated Army, 8-6, to cap an undefeated season. Roy Simmons's squad featured his son Roy Simmons Jr., Football Hall of Famer Jim Brown, Onondaga Nation faithkeeper Oren Lyons, and Jim Ridlon.

May 21, 1979—Syracuse's first appearance in the NCAA Tournament did not go well as Maryland rallied from a 10-7 deficit and went on to defeat the Orange, 16-13. Current SU assistant coach Kevin Donahue led Syracuse with 5 goals and 3 assists, Tim O'Hara had 2-5, and goalie Jamie Molloy made 21 saves.

May 21, 1980—The first NCAA Tournament game on campus at Syracuse was played at Coyne Field, and the Orange routed Washington and Lee, 12-4. Brad Short had 4-2 and Tim O'Hara 3-3, while Jamie Molloy made 20 saves.

May 26, 1984—Falling behind 5-0 in the first quarter and then losing leading scorer Tim Nelson to a knee injury in the second quarter, SU lost 13-10 to Johns Hopkins in the NCAA Championship game at Delaware. Tom Nelson, Emmett Printup, and Dave Desko all scored three goals, and Tom Nims set an NCAA Tournament record with 60 saves over the three games Syracuse played.

May 19, 1985—Tar Heels coach Willie Scroggs called this team his best ever at North Carolina, but it wasn't good enough to defeat the Orange in the national semifinals at the Dome, losing 14-13 in overtime. SU trailed 13-8 but scored the game's last 6 goals, including the winner by Emmett Printup.

May 24, 1986—Tom Korrie scored 3 goals to give him the all-time single-season record of 56, but it wasn't enough as the Orange fell 12-10 to Virginia in the national semifinals at Delaware.

April 11, 1987—Cornell ended Syracuse's thirty-six-game home-field winning streak at the Dome with a shocking 19-6 blowout, a precursor of things to come as a month later the Big Red ended the freshman seasons of Gary Gait and Paul Gait with an 18-15 victory in New Jersey in the national semifinals.

May 22, 1988—During a 23-5 demolition of Navy in the first round of the NCAA Tournament at the Dome, the Gait brothers combined for 16 goals and 7 assists. Gary set a tournament record with 9 goals and tied the points record with 12, while the team established tournament records for goals and margin of victory.

May 28, 1988—Gary Gait invented the "Air Gait" maneuver in an 11-10 national semifinal victory over Pennsylvania at the Dome, twice soaring from behind the cage to dunk the ball behind Quakers goalie John Kanaras.

May 28, 1990—The team that many believe was the greatest in lacrosse history capped its perfect 13-0 season with a 21-9 blowout of Loyola in the national championship game at New Brunswick, New Jersey. The Orange won its three tournament games by a cumulative 62-31. The 21 goals and 12-goal margin of victory were championship-game records, and MVP Gary Gait's 15 tournament goals were a record.

May 15, 1991—SU set a new standard for slaughter when it beat Michigan State 28-7 in the first round of the NCAAs. Jamie Archer scored 6 goals in the first half.

May 25, 1992—The Orange fell behind Princeton 6-0 and 8-2 in the national championship game but staged a terrific rally, and Tom Marechek's goal with less than a minute to play in regulation tied the score at 9-9 and forced overtime. After a scoreless first extra period, the Tigers claimed their first title when Andy Moe beat Chris Surran for the winning goal.

April 12, 1995—Playing as a Division I team for the first time, Hobart nearly pulled off a shocker before falling 18-17 to Syracuse at Boswell

Field in Geneva. Casey Powell scored the winning goal for the Orange with twenty-six seconds remaining and the win was the 250th of Roy Simmons Jr.'s career.

May 29, 1995—Syracuse had to play on Maryland's home field in the national championship game, but it mattered little as the Orange rolled to a 13-9 victory for their sixth title in thirteen years. Rob Kavovit had 4 goals and 3 assists, and goalie Alex Rosier had his third straight 17-save game.

February 28, 1997—In one of the wildest regular-season games in Syracuse history, the Orange opened the year with a 22-21 victory over Virginia at the Dome in front of 10,960 screaming fans. The Orange trailed 19-12 with just over 6 minutes remaining, but Casey Powell scored the last of his school-record 13 points when his seventh goal of the night with 2:34 left to play delivered the victory.

May 17, 1997—Casey Powell registered eight assists in a 13-12 quarterfinal victory over Loyola at Hofstra with Rob Kavovit and Paul Carcaterra benefiting with 4 goals each.

May 23, 1998—In the last game in the coaching career of Roy Simmons Jr. and the playing career of Casey Powell, Princeton dealt the Orange an 11-10 loss. Syracuse led 8-4 early in the second half and 10-7 in the fourth quarter but could not hold on as the Tigers scored the last 4 goals of the game and held the Orange scoreless over the final nine minutes.

May 31, 1999—Despite being seeded eighth, their lowest seed ever in the NCAA Tournament, the Orange defeated Princeton, Loyola, and Georgetown before the dream run ended with a 12-10 loss to Virginia in the national championship game at Maryland.

May 29, 2000—Coach John Desko captured his first national championship when the Orange routed Princeton, 13-7, at Maryland. Liam Banks scored 6 goals to win MVP honors, and Ryan Powell had 5 points, enabling him to tie his brother Casey for the all-time school record with 287.

May 26, 2001—Michael Powell's goal with sixteen seconds remaining in regulation capped a rally from an 8-4 deficit, but the Orange lost the national championship game, 10-9, when B. J. Prager scored for Princeton with forty-one seconds left in the first overtime at Rutgers.

May 27, 2002—Syracuse won its eighth national championship by holding on to defeat Princeton, 13-12, its third consecutive one-goal victory in the tournament. Earlier the Orange had survived against Duke, 10-9, and Virginia, 11-10, in overtime. In the finals the Orange held a 12-7 lead and with Michael Powell scoring 4 goals and 3 assists had just enough to pull out the victory.

Bibliography

Newspapers and Magazines

Baltimore Sun
Boston Globe
Buffalo News
Hartford Courant (Hartford, Conn.)
New York Times
Roanoke Times (Roanoke, Va.)
Rochester Democrat and Chronicle
Rochester Times-Union
Sports Illustrated
Syracuse *Herald-American*
Syracuse *Herald-Journal*
Syracuse New Times
Syracuse *Post-Standard*
USA Today
Washington Post

Wire Services and Web Sites

Adelphi.edu
Associated Press
Collegesports.com
InsideLacrosse.com
SUathletics.com
United Press International

Books

Macdonald, Rod. *Syracuse University Basketball: 1900–1975*. Syracuse: Syracuse University Printing Services, 1976.
Rappaport, Ken. *The Syracuse Football Story*. Huntsville, Ala.: Strode Publishers, 1975.

Syracuse University 2004 Football Media Guide. Syracuse: Syracuse University Printing Services, 2004.

Syracuse University 2004 Lacrosse Media Guide. Syracuse: Syracuse University Printing Services, 2004.

Syracuse University 2004–2005 Basketball Media Guide. Syracuse: Syracuse University Printing Services, 2004.

Waters, Mike. *Legends of Syracuse Basketball.* Champaign, Ill.: Sports Publishing, 2004.

Youmans, Gary, and Maury Youmans. *'59: The Story of the 1959 Syracuse University National Championship Football Team.* Syracuse: Campbell Road Press, 2004.